GW00836337

My

the

3 Continents

Kiran Wharton

MAPLE
PUBLISHERS

My Life in the 3 Continents

Author: Kiran Wharton

Copyright © Kiran Wharton (2023)

The right of Kiran Wharton to be identified as author of this work has been asserted by the author in accordance with section 77 and 78 of the Copyright, Designs and Patents Act 1988.

First Published in 2023

ISBN 978-1-915996-09-1 (Paperback)
      978-1-915996-10-7 (eBook)

Book cover design and Book layout by:
      Maple Publishers

Published by:
      Maple Publishers
      Fairbourne Drive, Atterbury,
      Milton Keynes,
      MK10 9RG, UK
      www.maplepublishers.com

Contents

The Beginning

My life started in India. I was born on 27th September 1954 in Karnal. A city in the northern region of Haryana in Punjab, India. I was named Ravinder Kumari Sharma. My dad, Ramtirath Sharma, was a teacher, and my mum, Kaushalya Devi, a housewife. I had four siblings. Three brothers and one sister. Harmesh was the eldest, next in line were Gulab and Ashok. My elder sister Maya was next. So, I was the youngest of all.

My dad had numerous transfers from one school to another during his teaching career. He moved from one town to another, taking along all his family wherever his post took him. But when I was about a year old, in 1956, my dad had a great opportunity to bring a great change to his life. He was offered a teaching job overseas, all the way in Kampala, Uganda, East Africa. My dad accepted this post. At that time Uganda was run by the British Government, and was recruiting teachers from various countries to come and work in Uganda.

My parents, along with all of us children, sailed from Bombay, all the way to the Port of Mombasa, which is located on the east coast of Kenya, on the Indian Ocean. It was common in those days to travel overseas on steamers, and when flying on a plane was not a common way of travelling. The journey would have taken at least seven days to sail from Bombay Port to Mombasa. Then a few more days to travel from Mombasa to Kampala in Uganda, which was done by train. My family must have found it strange coming over to a strange way of life to that they had been used to in India. An advantage for my parents was that my mum's uncle, her mum's brother, and one of her brothers, had already settled in Uganda, years before we arrived. After our arrival, my mum's younger brother ended up coming to Kampala, all the way from India. He lived with us for a while, then went to live with my uncle, his elder brother, who gave him a job in his business, which was in the building trade.

He later went his own way and became a welder.

My uncle came over to receive us, into our new way of life. In India, my parents had a simple way of village life. They had got married at a very young age.

My dad's father was also a teacher and my grandmother was a housewife. My dad had two brothers, but had lost their one and only sister to illness, in her teens.

My mum had two sisters and two brothers. She had had a very traumatic life. Her father died at a very young age. From what was told to me by my mum he was returning home from his work on foot. On the way he flagged a lift from a cart, which was being pulled by oxen. This was usually a form of taxi in their village in those times. He ran to jump onto the cart, while it was still moving. Unfortunately his dhoti (Loin Cloth) got caught on the wheels of the cart and he got trampled under the wheels, and that's how he met his tragic death.

As for her mum, she suffered a lot, losing her husband, and having to bring up five children was not very easy. Apparently my grandfather had a little Indian sweet shop in the village. After his death, some of the family members made my Nani sign the shop's deeds over to them. She being naïve and illiterate had no idea what she was signing. This would have been done by a thumb print, dabbed on an ink pad. Thus the shop was taken over by the greedy family members. My Nani got a very sour deal and was left with no shop or money, and was forced into poverty.

From what my mum used to say, my Nani would go to certain well to do neighbours, and Mill their wheat or corn on a stone, portable mill (chakki) and would be given a bit of flour in return for her labour. She was also known to have done some domestic work in return for food or money.

Sometimes she would hand-spin cotton into yarn on a spinning wheel. The material was called Khadi.

Khadi had been promoted in India by Mahatma Gandhi, who was encouraging Indians not to wear or buy foreign clothes. She had trained my mum in the art of hand spinning, so she would often help her.

My Nani was desperate to get my mum, who was the eldest of the five children to be married off, so that she would have less mouths to feed.

Her marriage was being arranged by the middle man to my dad, yet she was only twelve to thirteen years of age. My dad's parents thought that my mum was still too young to be married off, and also that my dad was still doing his studies, and would be happy to wait for a few more years, till the time was right.

To this, my Nani pleaded with my dad's parents, to take mum off her hands, to lighten her burden of bringing up the children, and explained her situation.

To this, my dad's family took pity on my Nani's situation, and agreed for the wedding to go ahead. He suggested that he would take in my mum as his own, and didn't expect any dowry. After the marriage, my dad would return to finish his studies, and that the newly married couple would be kept apart, till she came of age. So the wedding went ahead.

It is known that my Granddad was a very kind and well-respected member of the community. He was a teacher, he also practised Ayurvedic medicine. He had a little room in his house, where he mixed portions of natural herbs and roots. He had shelves full of various shapes and colours of little bottles, for storing his portions. There would be people coming to his door for portions of his medicine they believed would cure their ailments.

When my dad returned from his studies, and had qualified to be a teacher my parents started their family. They had four boys. Unfortunately, one of the sons died at an early age. Then came my sister and I.

In the Indian culture, it was known that it was a blessing to give birth to sons. Yet, after having had four sons, one after another, our grandmother celebrated the birth of my elder sister, by distributing sweetmeats to households in her street. She would say that the family had been blessed for a Devi (goddess) had been born in our family. She named her Maya Devi. The sad fact was that when one of my brothers died, my mum was with her mother. It was a custom then, that when a woman was in her last stages of pregnancy, she would go to stay with her mother, to be cared for till the baby was born. Sadly the baby died after birth, not long after, so did my Nani. She apparently died of a locked jaw. Not being able to receive any medical care caused her to lose her life. Not long after that my great Nani died too. So, my poor mum had three deaths in a row. That was a great trauma for her, losing three loved ones, one after another, in such a short period.

Thus, all my mum's siblings were orphaned. One of the middle sisters had already been married not long after our mum had, so she had settled with her husband. The youngest of her brothers and sisters were left homeless and orphaned, and ended up being adopted by one of the aunts. At the time her youngest brother was only a toddler.

The eldest of the brothers had ended up moving to Kampala, Uganda after their mum's death, to be cared for by our Nani's brother, who also gave him an opportunity to work for him in his building trade, and was also kind enough to send money over to the aunt in India who cared for the two young siblings, for their keep.

When our mum was in her last stages of pregnancy with my brother, Ashok, she had gone to the nearby pond to do the washing, as there was no running water in the streets. While she was there, she went into labour. Some of the women who were doing their washing alongside her had to take her home where she gave birth to my brother, with the help of a Dhai. The Dhai's were village elderly women, the Midwives, who had the skills of delivering babies. At that time most of the babies were delivered in this way. My parents lived with our grandparents, on and off, depending on where our dad had been deployed.

Soon my uncles too got married, and their new wives, also came to live with our grandparents thus extending the family. My mum and my aunts would do all the household chores and the cooking, and my gran would not have to lift a finger.

The village life in the Twenties, when both my parents were born, and the early Forties when they got married was a very simple way of life. Gradually my parents and the uncles moved to various parts of the country, wherever their jobs took them. This left my grandparents living by themselves, with occasional visits by their families, and with us visiting them, when on a leave after we had moved to Africa.

The Lower Flats

My memories of arriving in Kampala are non-existent, as I would have only been a toddler. But I do know that my parents were allocated a government flat. Most of the teachers and other individuals who had been given an opportunity to come to Kampala would have been moved into these flats.

These were three storey flats, in rows of may be about twenty blocks, with lawns dividing each building, and a concrete path leading to each entrance of the buildings. In the basement were store rooms, allocated to each household. On the front of each block, was a car park for the residents, and once again lawns leading from the front of the flats to the road. The whole rows of flats were secured with a high flint stone wall running from one end of the flats to another securing the flats from houses and shops behind them.

This must have been a luxury, compared to the life in the village in India, with all these amenities - running water in the taps, a bathroom with a proper toilet and a shower, a separate kitchen and bedrooms, and a large storeroom for all our storage.

Upon arrival in Kampala, my dad started his teaching job at Nakivubo Primary School, teaching woodwork and handicraft. He would also teach Urdu on occasions.

My brothers also got placement in the same school, whereas my sister and I were not school going age yet.

Then in April 1958, my younger sister was born. Her birth was at Mulago Hospital, in Kampala. The Mulago Hospital Complex was a teaching facility of Makerere University College of Health Sciences, and was the largest public hospital in Uganda. So, my baby sister was the only one delivered by a doctor and nurses, instead of a Dhai.

I remember my baby sister in a pram, and my brothers, wheeling her around, taking her for a stroll. She was so cute, we all doted on her. She was named Rakish Kumari. We used to play on the back lawns of the flats. I must have been about two or three years old, so wasn't able to take part in the games my siblings were playing, so I would just sit there and watch them play and sometimes wander off on my own. Once I got lost and ended up at the local Police Station. Don't know who took me there, or the ins and outs of the incident, but my parents had to come and fetch me. When they brought me home safe and sound, I boasted to my siblings that the policemen had given me sweets while I was at the police station.

I also had a habit of taking my shoes off, somewhere on the lawn and end up losing them. So my mum started putting me in boy's shoes, with laces, that she would tie up with double knots so that I wouldn't be able to remove them easily.

There is not much I remember of the times at the lower flats, as I was too young, apart from being so scared of a lady, who lived in the neighbourhood, who had sadly lost her young son. She had gone mental after his death and would go searching for him in the bushes, striking them with a stick, calling out his name over and over. I would run straight home, whenever I saw her.

Our family settled into a new way of life in the new country.

We were all given nicknames. Harmesh's was Bir, meaning big brother. Gulab's was Chinda, Ashok's was Shoka, Maya was Didi, meaning big sister, Rakish's was Poly and mine was Binder.

Our Journey back to India

In 1959, my parents took a leave, to go back to India, to visit the family they hadn't seen for so long.

The rule was, that if you took leave over six months, one had to give up the flat provided. All the belongings would have to be put into storage, till your arrival back to the country, and then be moved into a new property.

The leave was all paid off by the Government, the travel expenses, as well as the hotel accommodation. We travelled by train from Kampala to Mombasa. Then sailed from Mombasa to Bombay. Harmesh and Gulab had to stay behind, as they could not afford to miss out on their studies. They stayed with my mum's brother. My uncle would drop my brothers at school, before going to work. There came a time when both my brothers would be late for school, and get into trouble with the teachers, as my uncle would take his time getting ready for work, so my brothers' cunning plan was to set our uncle's clock forward so that he would have to get up earlier than he had to. This plan soon failed, as our uncle found out about what they had done when he ended up getting to his appointments early.

The memory of our travels is very vague, as I was too young to remember details, but what I remember is that my mum had filled large tin containers of homemade snacks for the journey. We would all gather around on the upper deck and share these snacks. Once again at night most families would gather on the upper deck, to get to know other families, and make friends. They would form groups to play card games. It was a beautiful view, especially at night, gazing up to a blanket of billions of twinkling stars in the sky, and being surrounded by dark waters of the Indian Ocean.

My mum and dad had a cabin of their own, and my brother and sisters and I shared a cabin.

We would gather in the dining area for lunch and dinner, but in the afternoon, we would be brought tea in our cabin, with biscuits, which we would share equally amongst us. That was a great treat for us.

In order to pass time, we would play a game of Ludo that we had brought with us.

There were games provided on the ship's deck that we would also have a go at.

Most evenings, there would be a movie played on one of the decks on a make shift screen. We would all gather together, to watch it, which was also a treat for us.

On arriving at the Port of Bombay, we would all gather around to watch all the luggage being pulled up from a huge hole in the ship's hull, on huge rope nets. We would try to see if we could spot our luggage, which were large metal trunks that were full of our clothes and gifts for our family in India, and where our dad had painted his initials, R. T. SHARMA with some paint, through a stencil, in order to be able to recognise our luggage in transit.

Then all the passengers would disembark the steamer into a huge port, with the hustle and bustle, the noise and the chaos all around.

My dad, panicking, making sure that our luggage had arrived and trying to keep us all together, my mum trying to hold on to us, so we didn't stray. The coolie harassing him, bargaining, to carry and transport our luggage. Our dad somehow managed to find coolies that were reasonable. They assembled all the trunks onto a wooden cart that was pulled by them, to whatever transport was used, to take us to our hotel.

We arrived in our hotel, where we were to stay for a few days, then board a train to take us all the way to Punjab. We were very excited, to be staying in a huge hotel, and to be waited upon by the staff, and served amazing food. Our parents would take us for a walk or shopping in the streets of Bombay. I remember all the hustle and bustle, all the bright colours, and the aroma of the lovely street food. Bollywood music blaring from every corner of the streets, from the shops, and from people carrying a little transistor radio, hanging off their bicycle's handle bars. Beggars begging all over the place, some of them were little kids of my age. Every building wall plastered with giant movie posters on billboards.

I remember us going for a walk on the Juhu beach which was a short distance from our hotel. Most of the Indian stars were known to live around this area. We would have food, bought at the beach stalls. We would be treated to Pani Puri, which was a spicy tamarind water poured into puffed puris, filled with chickpea and potato mix. The vendor would pass us the Pani-Puris turn by turn, till we decided that we had had enough, for our mouth would be burning by now, from the heat of the chillies in the tamarind sauce. Though I must say it always tasted out of this world.

Our Journey to Punjab

After a few days' stay at the hotel we soon set off on our journey to Kot Kapura, in Punjab, by train which would take at least three days. We were in a sleeper carriage, where there was seating on each side of the carriage, and bunk beds, that could be pulled down from the wall, at night. As the train moved, from station to station, we would look out of the window, at the beautiful scenery. We would pass fields of corn, crops of yellow mustard carpeting acres of land. Sugarcane and various other crops spread out on fertile land as far as the eye could see. Farmers tending to them, hoeing the fields with ploughs pulled by oxen. We would see rivers, lakes and ponds, passing us by. When the train was travelling on a bend we could see a trail of almost 50 carriages proudly being pulled by the engine that was run by coal. If the window was pulled down, and we were sticking our faces out of them, our faces would go black from the soot from the engine's coal.

There was always music playing in the background in our carriage, on a portable tape recorder my parents had taken with them, blending into the sound of the heavy wheels of the train speeding on the rail tracks.

Every now and then the engine would blow the whistle. Some of the poor families lived by the rail tracks, in makeshift shanty houses, waving at us as the train went past them.

Every now and then, we would approach a station, where we would witness a man feeding the engine gallons of water, by the aid of hand pumps, pumped from large water towers. There would be bundles of post being thrown into one of the carriages, ready to be dropped to various villages and towns.

Once again there was hustle and bustle at the station. People jumping in and out of the train. Everyone seemed to be in a hurry, the coolies carrying large trunks and bags on their heads for passengers.

My dad would get off the train, to get us some snacks and tea. The tea would be served in clay cups, and once the tea was consumed, we would throw the clay cups out of the moving train, trying our best to aim at some tree or post, and hear them crack in order to amuse ourselves.

It was a great adventure for us, this train journey.

Kot Kapura

We arrived at our destination in Punjab, in the city of Kot Kapura, about 50 kilometres from, Bathinda. The place where I was born.

Kot Kapura was a historic city, which takes its name from its founder, Nawab Kapur Singh. A nawab would be a sovereign ruler and Kot, meaning a small fort.

We were met by our uncle at the Railway station, welcoming back the family he hadn't seen for at least three years. We were taken to our grandparents' house, on rickshaws, with a couple of rickshaws carrying our luggage, following us.

The house was made out of brick, the walls plastered with clay and straw. The main door was a carved wood, with iron studs and plates embedded in for decoration, with an iron chain, on the frame, for it to be locked with a padlock.

Upon entering the house, there was a courtyard with a stone floor. A sitting room to the left. Followed by a kitchen, with a few shelves holding pots and pans. A few cupboards holding food stuff.

In a corner was a Chula (a cooking stove made out of brick and clay, like a barbecue). The fuel used for cooking on this homemade chula would be dried up cow's dung, mixed with straw, and dried-up sticks. In one of the corners of the courtyard was a water pump that would siphon the water from the ground when the handle was pulled up and down.

This was our source of water, for bathing, washing and cooking.

There was no toilet in this house. We had to go out to a barren land, where once an Old Fort stood. The Fort was long gone and this barren land was now full of stones and bricks from the crumbling walls, leaving just part of the ruins of the Fort standing on top of a hill.

A group of neighbouring women would gather up along with the children, head over to this barren land, carrying a vessel of water in order to wash themselves with. We would squat over to do our business. This would be done perhaps, once in the morning and once in the evening. The grouping of the women was done for safety reason as there was safety in numbers. It was a strange custom that we soon got accustomed to.

There were two bedrooms, past the courtyard. The first bedroom also had a storeroom where sacks made of jute stored flour, rice and various pulses. There were shelves in it too, which held various shaped, colourful bottles, which my grandfather used to store his medicines and potions, for his Ayurvedic Practice. The end bedroom was double the size of the first. It was held by a huge wooden pillar, right in the middle of the room giving support to the whole structure. The roof was held by wooden beams.

There were concrete steps going up on to the terraced roof where there was a Chavara (room on the terrace). As kids, we would mostly be up in the Chavara, playing games, keeping out of the way of the adults.

Some hot nights, we would set up our portable beds (Manji) on the terrace roof, and sleep under the blanket of billions of stars twinkling in the sky. Once in a while, we would witness a shooting star.

We were all to share this house during our stay in our grandparents' house. Though we would also travel around going sightseeing and go visit family and friends. On some instances, we would stay a few days with my uncles (my father's brothers), one of who lived in a place called Jaito, and the other one in Kapurthala. It was very exciting to meet and play and share stories with our cousins on these occasions.

Not long after we had been on our visit to India, my grandfather passed away. It was a sad time for my parents. My grandfather, had been the pillar of the household. He was also a respected member of the community. He was humble and kind, and always happy to help anyone that came to his door. I remember that he used to smoke a hukka pipe. There was always a sweet smelling aroma, of his hukka pipe smoke, lingering around us, in the house.

Once or twice, I remember taking to him, for his hukka, in a little earthenware container, some embers, that my mum or grandmother would have removed from the stove after the cooking was done.

My grandmother was a stern old lady. She was very tiny but with a lot of attitude. We, youngsters, were always afraid of her for she would scold us if we were to put our foot wrong. In her books, children had to be seen, not heard. So, we always had to be on our best behaviour.

We were not allowed to bring any shoes through the kitchen, especially if they were made out of leather, as she was a very strict Hindu practising woman. All our family members were brought up to practise the Hindu culture, but she took it to an extreme.

I remember accompanying her to a nearby place, where she collected some dung pats, for the stove, and despite being old and frail, saying that, I'm sure that she was only in her sixties at the time, but she looked very old. She carried a basket full of the dung pats on her head, balancing it with a cloth rolled up into a circle, to give support to the basket on her head.

I also recall, her having braids put in her grey receding hair, by a hairdresser. She would be sat on the steps of the front doorway, and the hairdresser would go through every strand of her hair to check for any lice, and once she was satisfied that her hair was clear of lice, she would braid it into neat vertical lines. This was merely to keep her head cool and tangle free in the summer months.

Sometimes, for our mid- afternoon treat, our grandmother would give us a small bowl full of corn kernels wrapped in a cloth, to be taken to the lady in the nearby street, who would drop the kernels in a hot sand pit, till they all popped. She would remove the puffed up white pop-corn with the aid of a large strainer, back into the cloth, that would end up being six times the amount we had taken.

We would all share them, with hot tea that would have been served in tumblers made out of brass.

Another treat we often had was the Kulfi from the ice-cream man, who would have an ice container on the back of his bike, carrying the Kulfi, which he would serve us in a piece of newspaper. On some hot days, we would listen out for the continuous ringing of the bell on the ice-cream man's bicycle as he entered our street, and ask our parents for money for the Kulfi.

Soon, our leave to India was over and it was time to leave our mother country, to go back to Africa. We were taken to the train station for our departure, by my uncles, along with the aunties and all our cousins for we would not be visiting them for a while.

As we said our goodbyes, the family members would start crying, as they embraced each other.

My sisters and I would try and bring crocodile tears to our eyes, because we thought that it was customary to cry, and we would be thought of badly if we didn't cry.

Return to Kampala

Once again our journey back to Kampala, would be by train from Kot Kapura, to Bombay. An overnight stay in a hotel and then sail back to Mombasa Port, and then a train journey back to Kampala. On our arrival, we were moved into a different flat. Once again this flat was on the Kampala Road, the same road as our first flat. We called these the Upper flats, and the old ones, the Lower flats. This was because these flats were built at a slope and the Kampala Road ran in the middle of the upper and the lower flats.

It was a three-bedroom flat, with a shared lawn in the front and back. It was the same design as the lower flats. There was an entrance to the front and the back of the flat. Top of each staircase, on the front of the flat was a rubbish chute located, where we would throw our rubbish, which would drop into a large bin, located in a bin shed, at the bottom of the flats, ready to be collected by the bin men. At the top of the roof was a terrace running from one end to another, with safety railings installed all around it.

All our belongings were brought out of storage, and our parents set up our new home again.

I have more memories of the Upper flats, than the Lower flats, as I was getting a bit older, and able

To remember things.

As I turned five years of age, I started school.

It was the same school as where my dad was a teacher, and also, where my brothers and elder sister had started their schooling. Though by the time I started my schooling, my brothers had already moved to Secondary schools.

My very first day at school almost turned into disaster. As Didi and I were walking to school, I was holding a brand new sharpened pencil that was given to me by my parents to start my first day at school. I tripped over and fell, missing my eye being punctured by inches with the sharp end of the pencil.

Our mum had never walked us to school, and we were independent enough to walk by ourselves, or with other children, from our neighbourhood.

Nakivubo Primary School was a well-designed school.

The Main headmaster's Block stood, right in the centre, overlooking a perfectly manicured lawn. It had a staffroom, and the bursar's office. The daily morning assembly and most activities would take place on the lawn. In one corner was the school bell that was rung between periods by one of the junior staff members. At the end of the school time, it would be a loud continuous ringing of the bell indicating that it was home time.

Along each side of the lawn were rows of classes, as well as some blocks of classes beyond the lawn.

The entrance from the main gate would lead into the carpark, adjacent to which was the playground where all the sports activities took place.

My dad was allocated an entire block, for taking his woodwork classes. It was as big as three classes put together. It consisted of all kinds of tools and benches and equipment needed for carpentry and handiwork. The best of the handiwork, made by the students was proudly displayed on shelves or in cabinets. I clearly remember one item. It was a grey wooden elephant which had a thin tube connected on the back. When some water was passed through the pipe, it would seem like the elephant was passing wee. It was very amusing to watch, especially as I was just five. Apparently, the idea was given to my dad by my mum.

There was another gate at the back of the school which we used, if we were walking to or leaving school.

There was a canal running across the boundary of the back gate, with a bridge for crossing over, from the school grounds to the outside.

As we came out of the school gates, we would come across the vendors, selling certain fruits.

There would be star fruit, corn on the cob, freshly cooked on Inghithi's and our favourite, which was green mango, which was sliced on all four sides, just enough to hold on to the stone of the mango. Then sprinkled with a mixture of salt and red chilli powder. This was a treat we always looked forward to while walking home.

As I turned six in 1960 my father bought his first car. It was a Fiat. My sister and I would get a ride to school on the days he was not going to school early.

Around our flats, my sister and I made lots of friends. Some were in the same school as us.

We were allowed to go out and play with our friends, for a couple of hours after school. And perhaps longer, at weekends.

I turned out to be a tomboy. I would climb trees, as high as I could. I would always be found on top of the boundary wall of the flats, what I believe was at least ten feet high, walking from one end to another.

I was always up to mischief, and had no fear of anything.

At the front of our flats, were rows of metal posts on each side of the lawn, allocated to each family, to be used as our washing lines. A wire or rope line would be used for this purpose, one end of the rope or wire would be tied to the opposite post.

I would end up going to a neighbouring flat and cut their rope line, in order to use it as a skipping rope or making it into a swing, which would be supported by the metal posts.

We didn't have any toys, or bikes to play with, so we had to find a way to entertain ourselves.

Every now and then the Council would come and cut the lawns on the back and the front of the flats, and the cut grass would be left behind. We would collect the grass and make little grass huts, using sticks, shaped into a dome, and then throwing layers upon layers of grass on them, then using these huts as our playhouses. We would use coco- cola bottle tops for our dishes, and a cotton reel for our stoves, in order to do our pretend cooking. There were certain eatable grasses and flowers that grew around us that we would use as our food.

There were always beautifully coloured butterflies, flying all around us. We would try and catch them by cupping our hands over them when they landed on the lawn or flowers. If we succeeded, we would tear the wings off and then save them, to place them between the pages of our books, and admire the effect of the pattern and colour they left imprinted on the pages.

That was a cruel thing to do, but at that time, we were ignorant and were not aware that we were killing beautiful creatures for our amusement.

We played games like Rounder's, Ring-a-Ring o' Roses, skipping, dodgeball, Hop- Scotch and Seven Stones. This game was played by stacking seven flat stones on top of each other, then with a small ball, taking turns to try and hit the pile till all the stones fell. The more stones that fell in one go would score the most points.

Whereas my brothers, who were older than us, played, football, hockey and various other games with their friends.

Once, one of my friends' mum had made her a rag doll, dressed in a beautiful pink satin dress, covered in beads, sequins and tiny little bells. I fell in love with her doll. I had never seen anything so beautiful.

She let me play with it for a while, and I wished that I could take it home with me, but she would not let me. I wanted it so bad that when I had the opportunity, I stole her doll, and threw it over the grate, that covered the storeroom below the flats, in order to hide it. My poor friend cried and accused me of taking her doll, but I denied it all. I wanted to play with her beautiful doll so bad, that I lied.

She went home crying, and I left the doll in the grate overnight, as it was too high for me to reach.

The next day, I used a long stick to release the doll and after playing with it for a while, took it back to my friend. I lied to her, and told her that I found it on the lawn. I couldn't have kept it, as my mum would have wanted to know where I got it from and I would have got into trouble.

There is another incident I remember, where my naughty part came out. My sister and I were with a few friends, and ended up climbing over the boundary wall that surrounded the flats, into the field at the back. This field was like a sports club where football, cricket, hockey and various games would be played. My brothers often went there to take part in such games.

On this occasion, we started watching the game that was going on. Then I noticed that the club shed door was open, and I noticed crates of fizzy drink bottles. We crept into the shed and each one of us helped ourselves to a couple of bottles. One of the blokes saw us and chased after us, but we ran as fast as we could, jumped over the wall, to the other side. The last block of flats, which was only a couple of blocks away from ours, where the tall wall got smaller, gradually, forming steps, is where we would ascend and descend from.

I was merely seven or eight years old, at this stage, and was getting up to mischief, but was lucky enough never to be caught.

Had the word got to my parents, about our behaviour, they would definitely have punished us and grounded us. But unknown to them, my sisters and I got up to a lot of mischief.

Every time we saw a police man walking by, we would shout "Askari-Jambo" to him, so that he would think that we were good girls.

I did get into trouble with my dad once though, when he had gone shopping and bought himself a beautiful watch. He showed it to all of us, let us hold it and admire it, and then placed it back in its case and then safely in his drawer.

We all sat down to have our dinner.

I rushed my dinner and excused myself. Ended up, straight into the drawer where my dad had placed the watch. Took it out of the case, and was looking at it admiringly, when my dad came into the room and saw the watch in my hand.

That was the first and last time I had a beating from my dad. He said that he had let every one of us have a good look at it. There was no reason for me to go back and take it out of the box.

At one time we ended up, a few flats away, where stood the largest mango tree in the neighbourhood. People would pick the mangoes as soon as they ripened, leaving the top ones, that they were unable to reach.

We would aim at them, throwing sticks and stones hoping they would fall. Sadly on one occasion, as one of our friends tried to aim a stone at some mangoes, it came down and landed on Maya's head, causing a cut on top of her head. There was blood running all over her long hair. She was screaming in pain, but we were so scared to go home to our mum as she would have scolded us for being so careless, so we ended up going to our friend's house, where her mother washed and dressed the wound. Then she took us home and explained to our mum as to what had happened. As it came from her, my mum was sympathetic and fussed over my sister.

One of my memories is that of when the ice cream van would drive up our road playing a tune, which went "Ting- Tong-Ting- Tong, Ting- Tong-Ting -Tong", we would run home and ask our dad

For some money for a "Ting-Tong" ice cream.

Each year we would celebrate Diwali, the festival of lights. It was a great time for us, as we would be treated to new clothes, and colourful plastic or glass bangles for our wrists, for the occasion. Like most Indian households, our house would be lit with Divas, little cups made out of flour dough, and then filled with ghee and lit, with the wick made out of rolled up cotton wool.

My parents would buy us fire crackers, bangers and sparklers.

Most of the kids would gather on the lawns, outside our flats and let off their sparklers and fire crackers.

My brothers would handle the bigger bangers, which made a loud banging sound when set off. They would light a banger, then quickly cover it with an empty tin can which would make the banger make a loud sound and the tin shoot up in the air, like a rocket.

My mum would spend days making heaps of sweet meats, and savoury snacks for Diwali. These would be served to guests, if they came over with their good wishes.

Sometimes, she would prepare plates full of the sweets, and these would be exchanged with friends and families. We always looked forward to see what the other families had placed on their plates of offerings. If there were to be small babies or kids in family, then a small toy would be placed with the offerings.

Our Cousins

Our aunty, mum's younger sister, came over from India to join my uncle, her husband who had already come over to Uganda to look for work, some years back. She had two daughters. We were so pleased to have cousins over, whom we had never seen.

We would play together, and listen to their stories about India. My Didi, my younger sister Poly and I, along with my cousins would end up together in the bathroom, which was a wet room, and took turns to get under the shower and sing a song. It was a treat having our cousins, who were same ages as us, come stay with us.

We would also end up preforming, dancing and acting, pretending to be the heroines in the movies we had seen, with an audience of kids watching us, sat on the stairs to the flats, using them as seats. They would clap and cheer, if they found us interesting. Didi was a very good dancer, and was admired by all the kids. She was very fair and beautiful, always favoured by all the kids. I didn't have any friends as such, I just shared her friends with her. Soon after a short stay at our flat, my aunty and my cousins moved into their own home.

Tommy

At some stage, we had a puppy. We named him Tommy. Tommy was an Alsatian, with a black and white coat. He lived in a wooden den outdoors, beneath the window of our flats, tied to a long chain, so that he could wander around easily. My brothers would place a bowl of water by the den for him and feed him too. My parents did not want the dog in the flat. Though my brother, Gulab, would often sneak him into his bed, without their knowledge, so tempted to play with the cute little puppy. My brothers were the ones to care for Tommy, took him for walks, and played with him.

Harmesh

In the year 1963, my eldest brother Harmesh had finished his schooling, and went into a teaching job in a local school till he was sent to England by our parents to do his further studies. He studied Accountancy in a University in Cardiff. When he completed his studies, he moved to Stoke-on-Trent to work for a South Wales finance company which was for Coal Board. We all went to the Entebbe Airport to see him off to his plane journey to England, where he would have to begin a new way of life amongst strangers and a completely different culture to what he had been accustomed to.

In those days, there were not many Asians about, so it was also difficult to find Asian food in the shops. He had to make do with whatever was available and adapt to a new diet.

We missed him a lot. My parents would receive frequent air mail letters from him, which would take at least two weeks to arrive from the time he had written them.

Every time my sisters and I saw a plane flying overhead, we would wave at it, pretending that Harmesh was on it, waving back at us.

Trip to India

In the year 1966, it was time to have another leave to India. This time my brothers, Gulab and Ashok, accompanied our parents, along with my Didi, Rakish and myself. We made the same journey. From Kampala to the port of Mombasa, and then by train from Bombay to the Punjab.

On our journey, we also stopped at the Islands of Seychelles. We spent a few hours walking on the beautiful sandy beaches, and my parents bought some trinkets, and gifts beautifully carved or made by the locals. It also docked at the port of Porbandar, which was about 355 nautical miles to the Bombay harbour, in order to drop off and pick-up passengers.

On our stop at Bombay, we would go to the Juhu Chowpatty Beach, where we would have street food, which tasted out of this world. Especially the Golgappa's, also known as Pani Puri. We would walk in the streets of Bombay shopping for gifts and souvenirs in the shops full of bright colours, in the hustle and bustle of traders, shoppers and shopkeepers, different sounds and smells filling up the hot and humid air of the harbour town.

Sometimes my parents would plan to go shopping on their own, and leave my brothers to look after us, younger siblings. We would play cards and amuse ourselves with board games. I used to love standing on the balcony, watching the locals going about their business. There were buildings being built around our hotel. We would see men and women labourers, carrying cement filled containers on their heads, climbing up scaffolding made out of trunks of trees, and ladders made out of bamboo, labouring hard from dawn till dusk.

At the end of the day, at night fall, there would be rows of people sleeping on the foot paths, in the shop doorways, on makeshift beds. Some families huddled up together to keep warm.

When in Bombay, we went to the Bollywood studios, to watch a film shooting which had been arranged by one of my mum's family members, an uncle who was a doctor at the Bollywood site. We managed to see many of our favourite actors and actresses.

On this leave, my father had planned to build a house, right next to my grandparents' house.

After my grandfather's passing, my dad got a share of the property. He had inherited the part of the property, attached to the main house, where previously the cows were kept for milking, and had not been used, for a long time. My dad decided to build a house on this part of the property.

The building work started, as soon as we got there.

It didn't take long to demolish the old cow shed, and soon the foundations went up. All the building materials like sand, cement and bricks would arrive on donkey's back. We would feel sorry for them, as they arrived laden with the heavy materials and could hardly move with the heavy burden. My dad's idea was that whenever we were to visit the family, we could live in the new house, as the family was growing.

He had shipped, from Africa to India, some of the items like a fridge, a sewing machine, a juice making machine, a new iron, some bed frames and several other items, that might come in handy, when the house would be ready to move into.

We saw the house being built, brick by brick. There was always chaos, all around us. It was still being built, when we had to end our leave.

One of our uncles took charge of the builders, and my dad was to send money over to him, from Africa, as and when needed, for material and builders' costs, till the completion of the house.

A New Home on Kampala Hill

When we returned to Kampala, after our leave, we were once again offered a new property. Our new house was a beautiful bungalow, situated over the Old Kampala hill, one of the seven hills Kampala was built on. It had three bedrooms, a sitting room, a dining room, a kitchen, next to which was a storeroom for all our cooking needs and for storing food. Through our bedroom, that we three sisters shared was a bathroom, which was really a wet room.

We would use a bucket and a jug in order to wash ourselves, sat on a low wooden stool. We would use Lux soap, to wash our body and hair.

Through the backdoor of the bathroom, was the outside toilet. Even though this was outside, there was a corrugated roof protecting it from rain, and thus was linked to the house. There was also a little concrete slab built outside, next to the bathroom, where we would wash our clothes, using a wooden cricket bat like aid. There was an outside tap there, too, which could be used for the washing purpose, and using a hosepipe for watering the plants in the garden.

There was also a garage in the drive, with a coal storage shed, adjoining it.

There was a path, with some steps, that led from the drive to the house. On the front door, my dad had screwed on his initials and his surname with chrome letters, proudly displaying R. T SHARMA. Most of the people liked having their name plate displayed on their front doors. The front of the house, had a lawn with borders of rows and rows of plants with colourful flowers, like marigolds, Lantana Camara and various other flowers that carpeted the whole of the length of the house.

On one end of the house was a large rose garden, with all the beautiful colours and scents. There also stood a Frangipani tree with its beautiful yellowish-white flowers that filled the air with its perfume. On the left side of the house there was a lawn, which was on a large mound with two sets of steps leading to the house. On the back of the house was a large patio, which was in two tiers. There stood a large mango tree, on the patio, and next to it a jackfruit tree.

There was always an abundance of the mango crop, when in season.

There were steps leading to yet another lawn on top of which were two boys' rooms and a squat pit toilet, and yet another lawn running the whole length of the house.

We had installed a washing line, one end to another, on this lawn to hang all our washing.

On one end there was a vegetable patch, and the other end, the hedge dividing our neighbour's garden from ours. At the back of the toilet, was a herb garden.

There was a single papaya tree growing by the boys' rooms.

This was a beautiful house. My mum would spend hours tending to the plants and my brothers would mow the lawns with a hand push mower. Thus the gardens always looked lush.

We had so much space for playing, and for our parents, for entertaining their guests.

The Nakivubo Primary school was just about a mile and half from our new house. My Didi and I would walk to school, sometimes accompanied by our cousin sisters who lived not far from us. Sometimes, if my dad was leaving school the same time as us, we would get a ride home in his car.

While we were growing up, we were brought up amongst different communities, such as Muslims, Gujratis, Punjabis and Africans. We picked up all these languages, along with Swahili which was the local language used by the Ugandan Africans.

We learned to speak Hindi by watching Bollywood movies. At home, we all spoke Punjabi.

We would accompany our parents to the movie cinemas, every time a new film was released. Soon there was a new Drive-in Cinema built in a quiet location of Kampala. It had a huge screen and could accommodate a few hundred cars.

Our parents would often take us to the Drive-in Cinema whenever a new film was released. At the weekend it would cost a few shillings per person, but on Wednesdays we could have as many people as we could fit in the car, for a small fee. Sometimes we would cram in two families in one car. Once we had parked, some of us would sit in the seats provided in the middle of the Drive-in Cinema complex. Every car would have two personal speakers to be placed on each side of the car window. We loved going to the Drive-in Cinema. We would take a picnic with us and have it in the interval. Families and friends would drive there together and meet up or park next to each other, whenever possible. That was a great way to socialise and share a picnic.

The only thing that we siblings were not happy about was when just before the film would come to an end my dad would start packing up to go, to avoid the rush of all the cars leaving at the same time and to avoid a bottleneck situation at the exit.

We would crane our heads towards the screen, from whatever angle possible to catch the last glimpse of the ending of the film.

Life was good at our new house in Old Kampala. We had a lot of garden space to play. We would let Tommy off his leash and play fetch ball with him. He loved the freedom of being let loose. Most of the time, he would be tied on his leash, beneath the jackfruit tree. He had a wooden den, with his bedding for him to sleep on, rest and shelter from rain.

Tommy was brought up a vegetarian, as our family were vegetarians. We would feed him leftover chapattis, broken into little pieces, mixed with milk. We also fed him Ugali, which is a type of maize and cassava flour which is also a staple food of the Africans. Occasionally he would be fed some meat by one of our boys. A boy was a young lad, perhaps a student or a young man, who would carry out some jobs for a family in return for a place to stay. Having the two boys' rooms, otherwise known as servants' quarters at the top of the back of the house, one of which was allocated to the boy, and the second one was used by my dad as a woodwork shed and for all his tools for his woodwork. Having a toilet next to these rooms was convenient for the occupant of the boys' room.

The boy would be given some money to get some meat for Tommy from the nearest butcher. It would have to be cooked by him, as there was no way the meat would be brought into our kitchen, let alone cook it. He would boil the meat in a bit of water and when cool would feed it to Tommy, who was in heaven to get something so delicious. He would chew on the meat till every bit of meat was off the bone, and then spend hours sucking at the bone till all the juicy bone marrow was consumed.

During our time at our house in old Kampala, we went through quite a few boys. The very first one was a lad who worked at my dad's school. He had a daughter called Elizabeth of about 7 to 8 years of age, and my dad let them stay in the boys' room, in return for cutting the lawns, a bit of ironing, and odd jobs.

None of the boys ever worked inside of the house, most of their chores were done outside of the main house.

The second one was a student; his name was Dennis. He was studying in a local high school. He too did the same chores as the first one. He was an intelligent guy. He used to sit on the steps outside his room and play beautiful tunes on his recorder.

I remember an incident, when once our washing on the line had been stolen. Most of the linen in our house was white, and my dad's and brothers shirts were all white too. Both the white linen and the shirts had been stolen.

My mum was very distraught by the incident, as the cotton linen had been purchased in Bombay, on one of our trips to India, and were her pride and joy.

Dennis suggested that we hung some washing on the line and he kept an eye out in the evening, when it got dark. In case the thief returned, he would catch him. My mum hung out some old shirts, hoping the trick would work. He wore a black pair of shorts, and didn't wear his top, so that he would not be visible to the thief, in the dark, and would pounce on him, if he did.

But the thief did not return. So we didn't catch him.

We often went to visit my aunt and cousins who lived on the opposite side of the Kampala road, which was the main road that went up hill from the town centre to old Kampala, past the turning to Berkley Road, where we lived. Most of the essential shops were lined up on this road. There was a Sudan store that was like a chemist, selling medicines, toiletries, and beauty products. We would often purchase our nail polishes from there. As we entered this store we could get lovely scents of the perfumes. Then there was the Rosina Store that sold clothes and all kinds of household items.

My cousins were more or less the same age as Didi, myself and my little sister, Poly. So, we played games and had great fun at their house. Occasionally they would come and play at our house. We often walked to school with them as well. It was good to have our cousins to play with, as we were not really allowed to bring friends home or visit them.

My dad had loads of friends, mainly teachers. We would go to their house or they would come to ours, and if they had children, we would play with them.

My mum being a housewife, would keep the house, cook and clean. She took pride in keeping the house pristine. All our bedding would be white cotton, crisp and clean, always freshly pressed, before every change of bed covers. She would get on her knees and wash the floors with a hot soapy water and a scrubbing brush. Then wipe them dry with rags that were normally my dad's old vests. They always came out shining. We would help her occasionally, but ended up having more fun than work, by sliding on the slippery, soapy floor in our bare feet from one end of the room to another. Most of my mum's friends, when visiting her would comment on how shiny her floors were, and wanted to know how she maintained them.

She did all the housework in the morning, then most afternoons, she would go to various religious groups, with her friends. She was very pious, and practised Hinduism. Most of the walls in our living room and my parents' bedroom were displayed with framed, depicted pictures of most of the Hindu gods. She would often go to her friends', to a satsang, where the ladies would gather in a house that was hosted by one of her friends, and sing religious songs, based on Rama, Krishna and various gods. These were called the "Bhajans". There would be offerings of Indian sweets and fruit after every ceremony. All the women would take turns to hosting these religious gatherings. If we were not at school, we would accompany our mum to these gatherings. Just the girls though. My brothers were never keen to accompany us.

My mum would always dress us girls in more or less the same dresses, made out of material she would buy from the local haberdashery, made on her 'Singer' sewing machine with matching ribbons plaited into our long braided hair.

We had long shiny hair, due to my mum massaging our hair with warm coconut oil, then asking us to sit under the sun, for it to seep into our scalp and nourish our hair. We never had the need to use shampoo. We would just use Lux soap for our body and hair, and yet it would come out clean and shiny.

My mum had hosted numerous satsangs at our house, where a group of ladies would sing Hindu religious songs and play a Dholki, harmonium as well as cymbals and a tambourine.

One of the ladies would start singing, then all the other ladies repeated the lyrics.

She was very clever in the way that she used to create a religious song by altering a few lyrics of some Bollywood songs. She always made sure that they still rhymed. She would pick the most recent Bollywood song and spend hours preparing a new Bhajan, writing, and altering the lyrics in her notebook till it was perfect, days before a satsang was due, so she could surprise her friends with a brand new Bhajan.

There were various clubs, where she would meet up with her friends. The main one was an Arya Samaj, where a priest, or some religious body would preach.

We were once blessed with the Shankaracharya coming to our house. The Shankaracharya was the head of the monastery at that time in the Advaita Vedanta tradition of Hindu Dharma. It would be a great honour, such great being coming to your house. He had come from India, and his devotees were booking him to come bless their house. So, we were very lucky to be able to have him come to ours. Our house was prepared for him, with an offering of garlands made out of marigolds and banana leaves draped over the front door and the entrance. We had a house full of people with some in the street who had come to have a glimpse of the Holy man.

The Holy man would preach, and bless all his followers present before he left, with offerings of clothing from our parents and well-wishers.

There were times when my mum would do a "Saptah". This was once again a religious ceremony, where the Holy book of Ramayan would be read in seven days.

My mum would be up early in the morning, bathe and prepare offerings. Then sit for hours reading page after page of the Ramayan till sunset. She would read it aloud, instead of in her head, so that we could listen to her readings. Whenever we could, we would sit alongside her and listen to her read the stories about Rama and Sita.

After sunset she would offer sweet meats and fruit to the gods, before she had any herself. This would carry on for the seven days. Sometimes, my aunt would come over to listen to her reading, and take over from her to read, to give her a break. Sometimes my mum would lose her voice and she would end up with a hoarse voice from reading loud.

On the seventh day she would hold a satsang to complete the ceremony of Saptah.

That is when most of her friends would be invited over to end the reading of the Ramayan.

There would be a big vegetarian feast afterwards.

My mum was very creative. She was a great seamstress and would make all our dresses.

She was also an amazing cook.

She could knit, crochet and when she had been in India, she would weave rugs called durri. Some of her creations had travelled to Kampala with us, and were used as rugs.

My dad once had a private job where he had to make wooden cases that would then have radios installed in them. It so happened that my mum ended up making them, as she was better at making them than our dad. They were skilfully finished, with a couple of coats of varnish.

She also completed a few other projects for my dad.

My mum, despite having had no education, was able to read and write the Indian languages, like Hindi, Urdu and Punjabi.

She was a very strong lady, apart from the times when she would have some kind of mini seizures. Every time she had some kind of bad news, she would go into a fit and her body would shake and her teeth would chatter and she would go cold.

My dad would rub her hands and feet in order to bring some warmth into them.

We could not understand what was wrong with our mum, and we would cry, and panic, especially when my dad would tell her not to die and leave him on his own with six kids to support.

He would give her a portion of some ayurvedic medicine that he had brought from India, mixed in honey, and spoon feed it to her. That would often do the trick, and she would soon feel better.

Then he would give her some Glucose mixed in water, to drink.

My dad often tried to avoid giving her any kind of bad news, but sometimes it was impossible to keep it from her.

My mum always liked her legs being massaged, after a hard day's work cooking, cleaning and gardening, and not to forget, finishing our dad's projects. She would call one of us to massage her legs, or walk on her legs and back as she lay on her front, on the bed.

Nakivubo Primary School

My dad being a woodwork teacher, had his own block allocated to him. It contained all the tools you would need for woodwork and handicraft.

The woodwork classes were only attended by the boys, the girls had to do needlework. So my memory of the woodwork block is just passing by the block and looking in.

My dad was known to be very strict. He was referred to as "Bwana Khari'' by the students, in Swahili, meaning a Kingly Sir. He was also given this name, because he was very strict. It is known that he did not even spare my brothers, if he took their class, and they would get equal punishment, to any other student, if they did wrong. Though he was a woodwork teacher, he would hold Urdu classes, in place of an absent teacher. Despite this, he was well respected by students and staff.

My Didi and I would meet up at lunch break and hang around. Sometimes she would be with her friends, but since I had just started school, they were happy for me to join them.

We would buy boiled mogo (cassava) from the canteen, which only cost ten cents per portion.

My mum would give us ten cents each for our lunch. My ten cents that had a hole in the middle would be held by a safety pin and pinned on to my blouse.

We would take some chilli powder and salt sachet, to pour over our mogo, in order to make it spicy.

Soon, it was decided by the health council, that mogo was not very nutritious for the children, as it was full of carbs, and introduced soya buns and boiled peanuts to the canteen. So, there was a healthier choice for the school children. We were happy with the introduction of the two changes, as they were very tasty.

Every now and then we would manage to buy a bottle of Coca-Cola to go with our lunch, as a treat.

School days were good, I made loads of friends. Our classes of thirty students were of African

Muslim, Indian, Gujarati nationality. It was definitely a multicultural school.

As I got a bit older, and new subjects were introduced, instead of just painting, drawing, colouring and cutting shapes out of paper, and doing simple arithmetic sums, with the aid of an abacus, singing nursery rhymes. My English, Literature and Geography were average but maths and the science subjects very difficult to grasp. The maths was especially mind boggling. The figures put in front of me would just dance about on paper and not make any sense. My brain would boil trying to figure out how to solve the sums.

I wasn't any good at sports either. We would play dodge ball, Rounder's, hockey and volleyball.

I was no champion in any of these games.

Once, I was picked to join the Volleyball team, and had to play against another local school. We were walked to nearby Lugogo Stadium by our sports teacher and met up with the other school party.

The teams were picked, but I was asked to return back to school. I was not picked, as I was not tall enough, and had only been taken along as a substitute. Still, I didn't understand why I wasn't allowed to stay back and watch the game.

My Didi on the other hand was good at Hockey and Rounder's. She was a very fast runner and always good at scoring points.

Then again, like me, she was not very bright in maths and science subjects.

Some of our teachers would be a bit cruel to us, if we didn't do well in class. They expected us to be good in all subjects, since we were a teacher's kids. We would even get a slap or two, and a strike of the ruler on the palm of our hand, and made to stand in the corner of the class as a punishment. And surely the word would get back to our dad, in the staffroom.

Didi and I had to be at our best behaviour at school, in fear that our dad would come to hear of any wrongdoing on our part.

Whenever we sat our exams, we would struggle. Our result paper would normally show the percentage of marks we had scored. The pass mark would be marked in a blue ink and the fail would be marked in Red ink. Our result sheet would be full of red entries.

At the end of the school day, Didi and I would wait for my dad by his car. He would get in the car, with the two of us in the back seat, and ask us to show him the results. One glimpse, and he would soon notice all the red ink marks and would shake his head, and all the way, on our drive home, he would be repeating the words, "Maya failed, Binder failed", "Maya failed Binder failed" on and on, till we got home. We would be sat in the back seat with our heads down in shame and tears in our eyes.

When at home, my mum would hear of our bad results. So, for days, we would feel ashamed and sad, especially when they talked about it to their friends.

Rakish had joined our school too for a little while, but was transferred to Old Kampala School, the school Harmesh and Ashok had attended.

My brothers and my younger sister, Rakish, were bright and always did well at school. Somehow Didi and I lacked their brightness.

The fact that we missed a lot of schooling, when we went on our trips to India, didn't help.

Perhaps, we needed extra help or tuition, but never got it. We didn't have a mentor to encourage us to do well in our studies.

The teachers didn't care or help either. If a child was a bit slow at learning, they would not take interest in them and concentrate on the brighter pupils.

In our maths class, the teacher would teach us, the times tables in Punjabi, and not in English.

So, I have always ended up, thinking the times tables in Punjabi, and then converting them to English numbers.

I believe that my lack of grasping the school teaching could have been due to being dyslexic. But at that time, this would not have been recognised, and there would have been no help from the authorities.

It was a crazy system in our primary school. When I was about eight years of age, at that time, I had two sisters and their brother in the same class. The eldest, Salma, was about twelve, then the brother Badroo, about ten, and Zubeida, about my age. I used to end up sitting next to Zubeida.

She would steal my colouring pencils or eraser. When I asked her to give them back, she would turn to her elder sister and go, "Salma! Ravinder kupiga Mimi," meaning that Ravinder is hitting me, though I hadn't even touched her. Thus, instead of me getting my stolen goods back, I would end up getting a telling-off by Salma.

I had some strange habits of chewing on the ends of my pencils, and then eating the lead in the pencil. Though I didn't like the taste of the lead in the coloured pencils. I would also eat little pieces of white chalk, left behind on the blackboard easel by the teachers. Other strange habits were that I would go up to my dad's workshop shed that was at the top of the garden where he carried out his carpentry. If he had used Evo-stick, I would peel off the drippings of the dried-up glue on the tin and chew it like gum.

On our patio the house wall was painted in a whitewash. This paint would start peeling off with the sun's heat, so I would pick on it and almost ended up eating half the wall. Eating charcoal was yet another bad habit.

I loved climbing the mango tree that stood on our patio. I would climb as high as I could, sometimes swinging on the branches. It was quite large, and well established. Each year it would produce flowers, then the most delicious crop of mangoes.

Sometimes if it rained heavy, the patio would be scattered with ripened, golden yellow, sweet mangoes.

We would sometimes climb on to the tinned corrugated roof of the toilet, from there, to the top of the roof of our bungalow. We would lie on the top of roof, holding on to the ridge, from where we had a great view of the Namarembe Road and the parade of shops. We would watch the world go by. If ever we saw our dad's car coming up the road, we would slide down the roof quickly. Our clothes, hands and legs would go red, from the wash on the red roof.

We had the privilege to go on various school trips. One of them was to see the Owen falls dam in Jinja situated on the White Nile. This belonged to the Uganda Electricity Board. We were also taken to the Jinja cotton Mill, where we saw how the cotton material was made. There were rolls and rolls of various colours of cotton being produced on giant weaving machines.

These were used for making the school uniforms, and material for sheets and linen.

Then there was the Jinja Breweries that produced the Jinja Nile Beer. We were taken around the Brewery and all I could smell was the strong Pomba. Pomba was a word used by the locals for beer, or alcohol. One of our teachers gave us some hops to taste. I simply refused, as my parents were teetotal, and were against any kind of alcohol. I didn't realise at that time that they were just barley hops.

We also visited the Coca-Cola factory which was in Kampala.

My dad would often bring home some form of stationery from the school for us. May have been given to him by the Bursar, Mr Vagi Bhai Patel, who happened to be our next door neighbour.

Once he brought home a litre bottle of blue ink. He said that this would last us for month, as we used to use ink pens, and would syphon the ink straight from the bottle.

When he had put the bottle down on the dining table I was tempted to examine it. I picked up the bottle, but somehow it slipped through my fingers and smashed on the concrete floor by the kitchen. It splattered all over the walls and cupboards. Forget about it lasting us months, it was gone in a minute. I got a good telling off by my dad, and was on my hands and knees clearing up all the mess I had created, with tears rolling down my cheeks.

Mr Patel next door had a wife, a daughter and three sons. His wife would never come out and socialise, so we would only see her if we went to their house. But he would come out and chat to my dad, over our boundary fence. Every late afternoon, after dinner, they would both pace up and down his bit of the garden, which was just mud really, not a lawn. They would both chat for hours, perhaps about school matters. There were two huge trees on Mr Patel's side of the garden, where bald headed eagles would make their nest and circle around our houses. I was very scared of them and always hoped that they would not land near me.

One of his brothers lived opposite our Road. There was a muddy path that led to their house. They had a beautiful, large property. We often crossed this path, as a short cut to the road that led to a road we walked to our school from, and also backed the Khoja Mosque, which was called the Aga Khan Mosque.

His brother's family had some servants, and an 'Ayah' who was kind of a child minder. She would look after the children, while the lady of the house did her cooking or other household chores. The Ayah had a daughter of her own, whom she named Monday, and then when she had her second daughter, she named her Tuesday. We used to think that was quite funny.

No idea, if an arrangement had been made with Mr Patel but my dad used to drive his car from the neighbour's drive, through into the side of our house, through the gap between the wire fences, which divided our houses, in order to have it washed by my brother. He would ask one of us siblings to go borrow the Argus, which was the local newspaper, from next door. We would be so embarrassed to go and ask, as sometimes, he would say that he had not yet finished reading it. Then we would have to go back later.

My brother, Ashok, would often play cricket on their ground, with his boys.

The youngest son was about ten years old. He forever had a runny nose, so his mum would hang a handkerchief on his shirt with a safety pin and he would always be blowing his nose on it. The eldest of the sons had polio, and used to wear a brace with a shoe attached to it, yet that didn't stop him from running and making runs, when he was batting while playing cricket.

None of the members of Mr Patel would cross the wire fence into the boundary of our house, even if their ball had come into our garden, because they feared Tommy, who would bark like mad when they did. So, they would have to patiently wait for one of us to throw it back into their garden.

At that stage we didn't have a television. So, our dad had kindly asked Mr Patel if we could go and watch their TV. It was just us kids though, our parents didn't join us. We were cheeky enough to go next door to watch their TV. We would all sit on the floor, our eyes glued to the television.

We did that for a few months till our dad purchased a television. It was black and white in those days.

We watched cartoons, like Tom and Jerry. We also watched Bonanza, and loved little Joe in it.

Then there were programmes like Beverley Hillbillies, Bewitched, Count of Monte Cristo, Doctor Who and several other American shows. Our favourite programme was The Fugitive which starred David Janssen. There were only a few hours of television time scheduled each day. The end of the day would be the News, which my dad never missed. He was not interested in watching the programmes that we watched.

Our grocery shopping was always done at the local shops, and the vegetables bought from the local Nakasero Market. Which was also named the Sconi, where the vendors would make little heaps of various fruits and vegetables, priced according to each vendor and my mum would barter and buy a heap or two, of the desired vegetables and fruit, from whoever gave her the best price.

At the grocery shop, we would ask for the amount required of pulses, rice, flour, sugar, etc. All these ingredients were stored in jute sacks, they would be weighed on the scales and sold in paper bags which was annoying as the bags would split before we got them home. So, a very strong wicker basket was required to carry them. We would call these baskets "Khappu". The milk would be delivered by the milk man, who would pour the required amount from a milk churn, using a measuring ladle, into a pan. If we needed extra milk, we would purchase it, sold in triangle shaped pouches at the local shops.

There was a large supermarket in town, but food there was expensive. There were too many mouths to feed on my dad's salary. So, a trip to this supermarket was very rare. My mum was good at making the food go far by improvising with what she had.

She was a great cook. After each meal, my dad would praise her cooking saying that it was the best meal ever. He always preferred eating in, as everything would be prepared from scratch.

Whenever we helped shell the pea pods, we would start eating them raw. She would scold us and say that if we ate them uncooked, we would have trees growing in our stomach. That would stop us from munching on them.

Uncle and Aunty

My uncle, my mum's younger brother married a young girl from Kenya. She was the eldest of her seven siblings. It was an arranged marriage. He travelled to Nairobi along with members of our family to marry and bring back the new bride to Kampala. She was a very beautiful bride. Upon arrival to Kampala, the couple lived with my great uncle, till my uncle found a job at a stainless steel factory, where they were provided with a house, within the premises of the factory.

My aunty had an uncle who lived in Kampala, so her siblings would come and stay with him, and would sometimes come and visit my parents too. Her brother, Ashok, and sisters, Madhu and Bina, would make regular visits to our house.

When my aunty had her first baby, we adored her and loved carrying her around and playing with her. Once, during our half term, I was invited by my aunty to go and stay with her. I loved staying with her, as she would spoil me with treats. She bought me a most beautiful white dress which made me feel special. The first time I wore it, I kept admiring myself in the mirror, preforming a little dance in it.

My baby cousin was brought up on formula milk, which I discovered that I loved the taste of.

Once my aunty had gone to have a shower while the baby was asleep in her crib. I crept into the kitchen and helped myself to a scoop full of the milk powder. It was so yummy, so

I thought of having one more scoop. As I poured the powder in my mouth, my aunty shouted out to me, asking me to pass her the towel, which she had forgotten to take in with her. My mouth was so full of the dry milk, that I struggled to swallow it all in, before I handed the towel over. Luckily, she only opened the bathroom door slightly, so didn't notice the white powder around my mouth.

While my uncle was busy working in the factory, my aunty and I would take the baby out for a walk in her buggy. We would also take lunch for my uncle to the factory which was literally yards away from their house.

She would teach me how to read Hindi books for beginners, and the little Hindi I practised with her has stayed with me till now, and sadly I never progressed any further.

My aunty would often ask me to go and collect shavings of the fine steel from the factory, which she would use to scrub her pans with the help of detergent, till they shined like new.

She was a very kind and caring young lady and I enjoyed staying with her.

She was more or less the same age as Gulab, and still had a bit of childishness in her, but then that was her quality, especially among all the young children.

My Mum's Sister

My aunty had had three more daughters by now, and as they didn't live far from our house, we would often go to their house and play with them, or they would come to ours, and we would play in our garden. We would share nail polishes and eyeliners, to make ourselves look nice.

During certain religious festivals, we would gather in either of our houses and apply henna paste on our hands. Then when set, we would compare our hands, to see whose henna had set the darkest. The darker it was the better we felt.

We would sometimes meet up with our cousins and walk to school together.

My aunty would cook us delicious food whenever we visited her.

My uncle used to drive a pickup truck as he was in the building trade, and we had had a few rides in the back of his pickup.

We would often see him working on his building plans on large sheets of paper. We could not make sense of the lines and drawings on the sheets, whereas he would be engrossed in the drawings, planning his next projects.

His filing system for his receipts was amazingly strange, as he would feed the papers through a wire coat-hanger which had been straightened, and dangle them on a hook.

Secondary School

When I finished my eleven plus, I was to start secondary school. It was not a surprise that I did not perform very well at school and did not get the grades needed for my preferred schools, whereas my brothers had done well and were able to attend schools of their preference. Harmesh and Ashok had gained admission at a local, Old Kampala School, and Gulab in Kololo Secondary School. Both these schools were the best in Kampala.

I ended up in the same school as my Didi, as her grades had been poor as well.

It was an all-Girls' school called Arya Samaj School which was run by a monotheistic Indian Hindu reform movement. We had to pay a monthly fee, in order to attend this school, whereas the Old Kampala and Kololo schools were run by the government, and did not require you to pay any fees.

I loved my new school. I had some great teachers and made some great friends. I started picking up, on understanding the lessons. My favourite subject was literature. I remember reading "Sense and Sensibility" and "Pride and Prejudice".

I also did needlework and home economics, which I thoroughly enjoyed.

My best friend, in my class, was a girl called Nirmala. She was a beautiful being, very kind and loyal.

She had lost her dad, and lived with her mother, a sister and brother.

They were very poor. Her mum used to make Samosas (a vegetable filled pasty) and sticks of Candy Rock, or toffee from home, and sell them, in order to earn some money.

Nirmala would bring a bag full of both these items and sell them to the students in order to help her mother make ends meet. Sometimes, her samosas and candy were so much in demand that her stock would run out, and some of the girls would be disappointed that they couldn't purchase it.

After school, we would walk together, along with Didi and her friend to the bus stop, in order to catch the school bus home. I was so happy to have my own friend, for a change, as I had always shared friends with Didi.

We had another friend called Suda, who would often join us. She came from a very well to do family. On the way home from where the bus dropped us, we would pass her house, which was so grand. There would be expensive cars in their drive. In fact, we would often see her driving a VW Beetle. She was much mature and taller than Nirmala and myself, so I believe that she was older than us.

We were not allowed to have our friends come to our house, for some reason, so we would part company as we reached our house. I remember, on one occasion, Nirmala asked me if she could pick a few flowers from our garden for her mother. I happily agreed.

The next day, as she was passing by the house, she came into our front garden, and started helping herself to some blooms. My mum saw her picking her precious flowers, and ran after her shouting abuse. She was not aware that Nirmala was my friend, as she had never met her.

The fact was that my mum did not like anyone picking her precious flowers. They could only be picked by her for her god idols and for making garlands of marigolds and Frangipani, when she did her daily prayers.

The next day at school, I apologised to her for the embarrassing incident.

Another incident was, where my Didi was invited to join her friend and her Mother to go and watch a movie at the local cinema, which happened to be a Ladies' matinee show. She asked my mum, if she could accompany them, but was not allowed.

Her excuse was that we were always treated to watching movies at the Drive-in-cinema, so there was no need to go with friends.

Our brothers often went to the cinema with their friends, but our parents were very strict with the girls.

Whenever our parents went to visit their friends, we three sisters had to accompany them.

We were very shy. When offered any soft drinks or biscuits, we would always start off with a 'No'. We would look up at our mum for her approval, and would only accept the offerings if she said we could.

Then the host would always praise us for being such polite girls.

In our head we would be thinking, how much we wanted the coco-cola, filled with ice cubes and the yummy biscuits, the whole plate full of them.

There was one family friend of my dad, who at that time was the head of the Nakivubo School. We loved going to his house. His wife was a teacher in a different school, and they had two sons, more or less same age as us. We would be allowed to play with them in their bed room. We would join them in jumping on their beds, and have pillow fights, read comic books, like Bino and Dandy. We also played on a Carrom board with them. Their parents were so down to earth, that we always felt relaxed at their house.

Senior Secondary School, Kololo

My dad had a lot of friends who were teachers, so about a year after we attended The Arya Samaj Girls' School, my dad, with his influence somehow got us a place in the government school, which my brother Gulab had attended. It was called The Senior Secondary School, Kololo. This school had a completely different way of teaching to the Arya Samaj Girls' School. Most of the classes would be held in the class of the specific subject. We had a large Science lab, an Art room, a Woodwork class, but all the other classes were held in the main allocated class rooms.

We soon got settled in this school, and made loads of friends.

S S S, Kololo was built on a hill, so most of the classes were built on tiers. Right in the middle of each tier, on the top stood the Headmaster's Office and the staff room, with steps going all the way down to a space where the morning assemblies took place. On one end of the school was the canteen, where you could buy snacks and soft drinks. There were no hot food facilities, so we would buy the snacks and sit on the grassy lawns to eat our food, which was usually a packet of potato or cassava crisps and a bottle of coke. On the back of the school stood the most beautiful Botanical garden, where some of our Nature studies, and botany classes took place, and where we learned about the names of the trees and exotic plants and flowers.

Some lunch breaks, I would just go for a stroll in this garden with my friends.

My Didi and I had our own group of friends, so we would only see each other in passing. My class was a mixture of various nationalities and ethnicities - Indians, Africans, Muslims. I had a classmate who had come from Norway and one from Israel. She would talk about her escape from the war with Egypt, Soviet Union PLO and Jordan, and all the fighting and killings that had taken place.

Her stories were terrifying and unbelievable, and yet true.

Then there was a girl from Mauritius, her name was Laurett. Her older sister was in our school as well. Her name was Juliet. They had both come from Mauritius. I used to hang around with Laurett, Ranjeet, and a few other girls. But Ranjeet was my best mate. Michael, our class prefect would also join our group at lunch breaks. He was a African Christian, he always made us giggle with his pranks, and annoy us by pulling our hair, or tying our braids to the back of a chair when we were unaware. One day I decided to play a prank on him.

The boys' uniform was white trousers or shorts and a white shirt. I sat at the desk behind him in one of our classes. Before he had a chance to sit down, I squirted blue ink, from my siphon fountain pen, on to his seat. He was furious when he felt the wet ink and his white shorts stained blue. I was not in his good books for a long time after that.

Once a new boy joined our school - an American boy, with blue eyes and blond hair. The best- looking boy in school. I soon found that my friend Laurett started hanging around with him. Soon she would not join our group, like she used to, but choose to be alone with Stephen.

One day, she did join us, and I heard her arranging a rendezvous at a famous bar, where she was going to introduce Stephen to her parents.

At that time, I was very surprised that her parents were happy to have their daughter have a boyfriend, and have a meeting in a bar, as both these things were in no way acceptable in our family.

Even though I was having a great time in school, I still wasn't doing well academically. I would enjoy the studies and grasped most of the subjects, but when it came to exams, I would do badly.

I would prepare well for the exams, I would repeat and practise over and over. I would draw diagrams or maps, on a mini blackboard my dad had brought for us. For geography revision, I would draw rough maps of the country, and try and fill in the names of the parts of the countries. For Biology, I would draw a human body and try and fill in parts of the body and the organs, till I got them all right and trusted myself to do well, but as soon I was handed the exam paper my brain would freeze.

There was once an incident, involving a class mate of my Didi, who was well known and the most famous guy in the school, because he played in a band he had formed with two of his brothers. They would often perform on the Indian Culture Channel on television. And also did shows and performances at parties.

He somehow managed to get hold of leaked Physics exam papers. His younger brother was in the same year as me so he got it for his brother and also offered it to my sister, for me.

I was handed pages of handwritten questions that might be in the exam papers. I looked up the answers in my text books and tried cramming them.

On the day of the exam, when the exam papers were handed over, I noticed that the questions were exactly the same as what I had been given. I got excited, and started answering the questions, to the best of my knowledge.

Later on, when the exams results were announced, I had still failed.

My brain had only grasped thirty percent of what I had crammed, the rest ended up in my brain's bin.

I was so embarrassed, when word got to my sister's friend who had given me the leaked papers that I had failed. His brother had passed with flying colours.

There was a time when the school prefects were being recruited. My friend, Ranjeet, decided to enrol for the position. Each candidate had to have at least fifty signatures from fellow students in order to qualify.

We both went around the school in our break times to get signatures. We got up to about thirty, when Ranjeet started to panic, and was not sure if she wanted to be a school prefect after all.

I kept on encouraging her, and talked about the great role she would be playing, but she had made her mind up.

We were having a group chat during one of our lunchbreaks when Ranjeet and my other friends suggested that I went for the role of a school prefect instead. "No Way," I said. That didn't help, because Ranjeet erased her name on the election sheet and put my name down instead. I tried to grab the sheet of paper from her, but she ran away with it. I chased after her, but my effort was in vain. So, I went ahead with their idea.

We only had to find twenty more signatures, which we managed and the sheet was placed in the election box.

I was very surprised when, in assembly, the names of the candidates were being announced, and my name came up as well. Like all the other candidates I had to walk up the steps that led to the top, where the Headmaster and the teachers stood, to collect a Prefect's badge, which would have to be worn on our shirt or blouse at all times, while at school.

I was in a shock, but also overwhelmed when I looked down from the top at the rows of students standing in perfectly formed lines, and clapping and cheering for the achievers.

Our role as a school prefect was to discipline our fellow students and make sure that they had the right uniform. Especially for the girls to have the correct colour ribbons in their hair, which were to be black, and check for girls wearing nail polish, or makeup. During the morning assembly, we had to stand facing the students, and after the assembly, make sure that they were in line as they dispersed to their classes, check for any rule breakers.

I was a bit mischievous, and yet a shy student. Not being very academic meant I was not the type of prefect looking out to put any students into unnecessary trouble. So just a little warning was enough, in my books.

I was challenged by my group of friends to do something about an incident when a student called Mohammed Bogardia was finding pleasure in throwing little stones at some of the girls in order to get their attention. I walked up to him and warned him to stop. He took no notice of my warning and later on started throwing stones at our group in order to spite us. Again, I warned him, and threatened to report him to the headmaster. To this, he challenged me to report him. My friends were goading me to report him. We both walked to the headmaster's office and I reported his behaviour to the headmaster. He was punished.

I was in my Art class once, doing a still life art of a hibiscus flower. Someone whispered in my ear from behind "beautiful work". I looked over, and it was Mohammed. That was it, he didn't utter another word and disappeared. I believe he was taunting me. I wasn't even aware and had never even noticed that he had been in my Art class.

The last time I ever laid eyes on Mohammed was when I was waiting at the bus stop, after school.

Standing there alone, minding my own business, when he appeared in front of me. He started pacing up and down, took one look at me and said, "You could be beautiful, if you didn't have such a large nose." I didn't know whether to take that as a compliment or an insult. I was not going to argue with him, I simply ignored him and got on the bus, never saw him in school or bus stop or anywhere else for that matter. I think he decided to keep out of my sight.

A couple of my friends decided to form a group that would spy on other students, and try and find out who was dating whom. We called our group 5-5-5. I decided to make some sort of a badge to represent us. I cut a round shape out of 555 cigarette packs, which was the brand of cigarettes famous at that time and stuck a safety pin on the back of them with the help of glue and we all had one each. It was all done in jest and a bit of fun, and the novelty soon wore off.

The bus journey home after school was always eventful. I would have to walk ten minutes, from the school to the bus stop. Then the bus would take at least twenty minutes to the town from where it would be another half an hour walk home. This was when my sister Didi had already left school, as she turned sixteen. When she was at school, we used to catch a lift from one of my parents' friend, who used to pick his daughter up from the same school. We had to sit on the back of his pickup truck. We were always embarrassed to be seen by our class mates, and would keep our heads down, not wanting to be noticed as we drove past them.

Going back to the bus journey, some of the naughty boys would ring the bell, but no one would get off the bus. This carried on for a few days. One day, when they did this, the driver stopped the bus and refused to move in order to teach the boys a lesson. It was only a stop or two from the town stop, so some of the boys decided to jump off the bus. I was worried that I would be late home, so I too left my seat and walked towards the exit door. Just as I was about to jump, the driver decided to move. I still jumped, while the bus was moving and fell on the path, all my books scattered around me, ended up with scrapes on my knees, all the kids on the bus cheering me. But I was so embarrassed. I would often walk to school on my own as all of my school friends lived near the school. My classes would start in the afternoon, from one pm to five pm. I would leave home at twelve pm, just as the local Indian radio channel would start reading the news, followed by playing of the latest Bollywood songs.

On the walk to the bus stop towards the town, I would hear the songs blaring out of people's properties. I enjoyed listening to the songs, which I would hum in my head all the way to the bus-stop. Then I would catch my bus to school.

My best friend, Ranjeet, lived in Kolola. So, some break times, we would walk to her house to have lunch.

She lived in a beautiful house. Very well furnished. I could tell by her parents' house, that they were well to do. Apparently, her father used to go hunting. In her living room they had four elephant's feet turned into stools. She told me that they were made from the elephant's feet that her father had killed whilst hunting. There were also heads of various animals hanging on the living room walls, preserved by taxidermists. I wasn't impressed that the animals had been killed, I felt that it was cruel to kill animals as a sport. But in those days, this was a common practice, amongst the rich and the wealthy.

Safari

During the term's end, my parents would take us on a mini break to Kenya, and from there we would go to Mombasa. We would travel in dad's Fiat. We used to call this our Safari holiday, because while travelling through various towns on the way to Kenya and Mombasa, we would travel on muddy roads, and at times come across a pride of lions, see giraffes wandering around, elephants and various other animals that roamed in the grassy verges of the road. If the animals were too close to the road, we had to immediately stop, and stay in the car, with the windows closed and the headlamps switched off, if it was dark, till it was safe to continue the journey. Our car would be covered in red dust from the muddy roads. We would have a welcome break for refreshments at the little towns that we passed where we would also get the car filled up with petrol, add water in the radiator of the car and do a mini check-up, so the rest of the journey would be safe.

The towns we would pass would be Jinja, Tororo then end up in Malaba, the border to Kenya.

From the border we would pass through Eldoret, Kisumu, Nakuru and then end up in Nairobi, where we would stay a few days at one of our family members'. We loved stopping there, as my uncle ran a fruit and vegetable shop, so we were treated to grapes and apples daily. In fact, they lived in some flats in the town centre. Their flat occupied the whole of the top floor. At the basement was a large cold storage, where all the fruit and vegetables were stored. My uncle would take us there sometimes. As soon as we went in, we would get an aroma of fresh apples, and a sudden coolness of the cold store. When we left Nairobi to go back home, our uncle would give us a case of apples to take with us. They would last us for weeks.

Mombasa was a beautiful sea side place we loved going to. We always went to the Bamburi beach, along the coast of the Indian Ocean. We would stay at a lodge and spend most days by the seaside.

My dad loved travelling and going places, so we were lucky to visit various parts of the country. We were also taken to Masindi, to the Northwest of Kampala, to the Murchison Falls, which is a waterfall between Lake Kyoga and Lake Albert on the Victoria Nile in Uganda. We would stand at the top and look down the lake, where the falls ended and sprayed us with fine droplets of water, which were welcome in the sweltering hot weather.

At the bottom, we would see great numbers of crocodiles basking in the heat, some with their mouths wide open, revealing their sharp teeth.

Our favourite place to visit was Entebbe, where the main airport was located, in Kampala, on the boundary of Lake Victoria. This was surrounded with botanical gardens, and beautiful open grassed areas, where families went to have a picnic, and have walks in the botanical gardens. There were huge vines hanging from giant trees that we would swing on like the monkeys do. The place was full of palm trees, where the small nuts would fall, as they ripened. We would collect these nuts, then crack the hard shells with a stone and eat the sweet nuts.

We often went to picnic at Entebbe with a few other family friends and relatives in big groups.

We would take a primus stove, which was fuelled by kerosene for cooking, and all the cooking ingredients. Some of the older children would shield the stove from the breeze, by holding the Makaka (a straw beach mat) so that the flames did not get blown out. Then all the mums would get together and come up with deliciously hot food. We all shared the food, and then went for a dip in the lake and splashed about, while all the ladies cleared the picnic, and the men played card games, often shouting in excitement if they were to win the game.

Our dad was in his element, when amongst his friends, enjoying his card games and having a banter amongst his mates.

Our House

At home, even though we had a well-equipped kitchen with an electric cooker for cooking, some days my mum would do the cooking on the patio. She would use a primus stove or an Inghithi, which was a round iron-stove, with a grill, fuelled by coal, just like a mini barbecue.

This was ideal to be cooked upon outside due to the smoke it would produce.

We spent a lot of time on the patio, entertaining family friends, playing and sometimes studying.

Once I was sat on a chair, at the patio doing my homework, when I heard a ruffling noise up on our mango tree. I looked up, and suddenly a couple of flat lizards fell, with a thud, just by my feet. I screamed and ran indoors. Despite living in Africa, I was always scared of reptiles and creepy- crawlies. My worse phobia was, and still is, of snakes.

During the rainy season, there would be a plague of green grasshoppers. These would swarm round and round the street lamps. In fact, they were everywhere you looked. If we were to be in my dad's car, during the plague, they would land on his windscreen. He would have to let his wipers run as fast as they could, in order to get rid of them. My sisters and I would close our eyes, as we didn't want to see them. They would also settle on hedges, plants and the long grasses, and would fly off when disturbed. That used to make me scream and run for my life.

Luckily, the plague was short lived.

We would have to leave all the doors and windows shut, during the plague, but a few of them would still end up in the house. We would try and get rid of them, by hitting them with a broom.

The Native Africans were delighted to have the grasshopper season, as it was a delicacy for them. They would grill the insects and eat them.

The worst of all were cockroaches. When we lived in the upper flats, I would get up to go to the toilet in the night. In order to get to the toilet, we had to go through the kitchen. As soon I put the light on, I would see all the cockroaches suddenly spread around the kitchen floor and hide under the cupboards. I would run back to the bedroom and wake my Didi up, too scared to go by myself. I would whisper in her ear, "Didi Dudoo!!" As if the cockroaches would hear us. We would both tip toe through the kitchen, in case the dudoos came back from their hiding places.

On the main road, that led to Berkley Road, where we lived was a beautiful Khoja Mosque. It was also known as the Aga Khan Mosque. The Khojas were mainly Nazari Isma'ili Shia community. The mosque had a clock on all four sides of its minaret. So, the time could be noticed from all angles. It would also chime every hour. In the evening, when it got dark, the mosque would light up with thousands of white bulbs that covered up every inch of the mosque. It was a beautiful sight.

As we lived at the edge of the main road, we would see the Khojas walk in groups to the Mosque, for their evening prayers. The men were always in smart suits and the ladies in beautiful dresses and high heels. They looked like film stars.

If by chance we had walked pass them, we would get a waft of their beautiful scent of perfume. We would consider them to be very modern, compared to the way our life was.

There was a big house, to the right of our house, it belonged to a family who ran a dairy. I believe they were Khojas as well. Their house boundary was surrounded with palm trees. We would go and collect the fallen little palm nuts. Sometimes the son of the owner of the house, who was believed to be deaf and dumb, would run after us, waving his fist at us, in order to chase us away. Once he made gestures of slashing our throat with a knife. We were very scared of him.

The strange thing is that as we turned into our teens, and happened to pass their house, he would stand in his garden watching us, and instead of scary warnings, he would gesture us to go to him. That was just as scary for us. The grassy area between their house and ours was used as a foot - path leading to the road to the back of our house. It formed a trail of worn grass which people had walked upon. We named this lane International Date Line as most lovers would end up there, found kissing and cuddling. We also took Tommy there for his walks so he could do his business.

Funny thing is that my dad would ring my brother, Ashok, from work or if he was out visiting friends, to make sure that he had taken "your brother" for his Poo! meaning Tommy. Ashok was the one caring for Tommy, till the time he too left for England for his further studies. Just like we had done with Harmesh and Gulab we all drove to the Entebbe Airport to see him off. Once he had passed the Customs, we saw him walk to the plane. We waved at him till he had boarded the plane and it had jetted off, to England.

He was met up by our uncle and was later picked up by Harmesh, to take him to Swansea in South Wales. He met up with our brother, Gulab, who was at the time doing his Engineering Degree at University.

He was then taken to Cardiff, where he was introduced to the family, that he would live with, whilst studying in College.

Not long before all my brothers left for England, both my uncles (mum's brothers) had immigrated to England. So, did my aunt's entire family and settled there. So, when my brothers went there, they had a family to visit, if need be, during their summer holidays.

Unfortunately, my aunty, was left widowed, a few years after they had settled in England, leaving her with two young kids, a boy and a girl.

By this time, my brother Harmesh had got married to a lovely young lady called Margaret.

They soon started a family, and had two sons, one of who's married and with two kids, a boy and a girl.

All my brothers, leaving for England, meant that all the jobs they did for our parents landed on us girls, like washing the car, taking Tommy for a walk, any urgent shopping my mum needed. I used to love cleaning my dad's car. I would sit in the driving seat, and pretend to be driving it. I believe that my brothers used to actually go for a little spin in it, without my dad finding out. But I didn't know much about the workings of the car for me to actually drive it.

Another job we were given by my dad was to clear the ash tray that had been used by one of his friends. He despised people who smoked, but did not want to offend his guest, and would put up with his smoking in our living room. If ever it was my turn to clear it, I would take it to the bin, but before disposing of it, I would break open the cigarette end and sniff at the tobacco. I loved the smell of it.

One day I decided to light up one of the ends and smoke it. I choked on the smoke, and yet loved the aroma of it.

An idea come to my mind, about buying myself a cigarette from the kiosk near our house, where you could buy a single cigarette, for about 10 cents. As I didn't want to be caught purchasing it, I sent Elizabeth, our Boy's daughter to get it for me.

I would light it up and have a few puffs, not even inhaling it in, but just producing smoke, so I could smell it.

I was so lucky that I never got caught doing that, for I remember when we were very young, my uncle and my eldest brother Harmesh had been punished by my dad, when caught smoking. It was a forbidden thing to do.

Our last trip to India

It was end of year exams, and I had been preparing hard to revise, day in, day out, hoping to do well. During my second exam, I was busy writing on my exam paper, when I kept having an urge to scratch my arms and chest, where I was itching like mad. I couldn't concentrate in the exam at all, and felt very hot and felt like I was coming up with temperature. I noticed that it was wet under my fingernails, when I had scratched over my neck and chest.

I had to raise my hand to get my invigilator's attention. As soon as she walked over to me, she noticed that my face was full of fresh blisters, and immediately knew that they were the sign of chicken pox. I had to leave the exam room and was sent home.

I did not sit anymore exams after that. Lucky for me really, as I would have failed in most of them anyway. Saved me from the embarrassment from family members.

The term came to an end and my parents, and we three sisters were to travel to India for our annual holiday.

I was full of scabs all over my body from the chicken pox, when we travelled, and was feeling conscious of them.

The trip to India was once again a similar journey as we had made on our previous trips.

This time my aunt, my mum's younger sister had accompanied us, though as we reached the port of Bombay, she had gone her own way from there, to go and see her side of the family.

My parents took Didi and me to various sightseeing places, like Chintpurni, Jwalaji and Kangra where we went to visit the temples of the Hindu goddess Mata. My younger sister, Poly, had to stay behind with one of my uncles, in order to and study and prepare for her forthcoming exams.

We would sit with the adult ladies in the street and chat to them, instead of playing up in the Chavara, now that we were in our teens. This holiday in India was once again a great experience.

Firoz

It was one late afternoon, when I was walking back home from school, from the road, back of the Khoja Kana Mosque, when I heard footsteps behind me. I looked behind, and a young man smiled at me and started chatting to me. He must have been about twenty-two or more. His dress sense was that of a Teddy boy. He had jet black full head of hair, with a quiff. He also had a goatee beard with a moustache, very well groomed. We walked together chatting, till I had to turn into a lane that took me home. He seemed harmless enough. I didn't at all feel threatened by him.

The next day, I saw him again at the same place. He was leaning against the wall, with one leg bent, supported by the wall. It seemed like he had been waiting for me. We walked, and chatted again till, once again, I turned into the lane, to take me home.

This carried on most days. I found that he was a Khoja, and attended the Khoja Mosque most evenings. I also found that he only lived opposite the main road to our house.

I got so fond of him, I felt that I had found a great friend to talk to. If ever he didn't come at the back of the Mosque to walk with me, I would miss him.

We would talk about the latest films we had both seen, about my day at school, by that time I would be at my turning.

He told me his name was Firoz, he lived with his mum, a brother and two sisters, and that his dad had died. He worked in a factory, to help the family financially.

One day, as I was walking back from the shops, running errands for my mum, I noticed Firoz, just as I was entering our house. So now he came to know where I lived. I would often see him walking on our road with his mates, perhaps hoping to see me. But that would worry me, I did not want my family to know that I was friends with him. That was not allowed. It was my secret. All my childhood, I had never been liked as much as Didi. She was the beautiful one and the favoured one. I was the one who tagged along with her. I was dark skinned and she was very fair. No one ever said that I was beautiful, none of the boys at school fancied me, whereas Didi had a lot of admirers.

So, when I got a bit of attention from Firoz, I felt liked and noticed for a change.

Eid was coming up, a festival the Muslims celebrate after Ramadan. I so wanted to get Firoz a gift for Eid, so I went to the Sudan store to look for a little something I might be able to afford. Everything was out of my budget of a few shillings I had, so I bought him a white handkerchief. I embroidered, the letter "F" on it and packed it neatly in a paper.

I also made him an Eid card, by tracing a picture of the Mecca, then sprinkled it with different coloured glitter, with the help of glue.

I handed it over to him, the next time I saw him. He told me that he would be going to the Mosque that evening, to celebrate the holy month of Ramadan.

I purposely went to the garden that evening, from where there was a full view of the main road, and watched all the

Khojas walking towards the Mosque, dressed in their finest clothes, hoping to have a glimpse of Firoz. They often walked down between six and six-thirty for the 7pm prayer. Then I saw him, hardly recognizable, in a smart suit, with a tie on. Walking towards the mosque with what I believe were his family members. It was only for a few seconds, then he was out of view.

I could imagine the whiff of his cologne lingering behind him, leaving a pleasant smell for the passers - by as he walked smartly dressed to his Mosque.

I decided to write him a note that night. In which I wrote, how I had seen him, and how smart he looked. Then I added some lyrics from a song, and drew a few hearts, in red ink. I folded it neatly, and handed it over to him the next time we did our walk. He didn't read it, just placed it in his pocket.

I went home, as usual. I was very nervous, as I didn't know how he would react to my note. After all we were good friends; was he even expecting a note from me with love hearts, neatly coloured in red ink?

I wouldn't be seeing him till Monday, after school, as it was the weekend.

Monday came. Walking home from school, I saw no sign of Firoz. I carried on walking disappointed, thinking what had I done! I should never have written that note.

I turned into the lane that took me home, then I heard a whistle, that sounded like a bird's sound.

I carried on, then heard continuous bird like sounding whistles. I stopped to see where they were coming from. It was Firoz. He got closer and was panting, as he had been running. He grabbed my hand and put a note in my hand. I went all jelly legs, as I felt his hand on mine. No one had held my hand before, apart from my sisters, or my mum. This felt different. He had a strong grip. He whispered that he would see me soon and disappeared. I went home shaking like a leaf, the note clenched in my sweaty hand.

It simply read Eid Mubarak! Then the lyrics of the same song that I had written to him. I was so happy, and yet terrified of what was becoming of this friendship we had. It was not allowed. He was much older than me. I was coming up to being fifteen, and he was over twenty-five. He was a boy and I was a girl. I was a Hindu girl from a respectable family. He was a Muslim. I couldn't sleep that night. I cried under my sheets, so that my sisters wouldn't hear me. What was I to do? I couldn't tell my sisters or my friends at school, because deep down in my heart, I knew what I was doing was wrong.

It was at school, that I wrote him a note, in case I saw him again that afternoon. This time I wrote some lyrics from a sad song and mentioned that I was scared and that we would have to stop seeing each other.

Walked home as usual, but no sign of Firoz. Walked up the lane towards the house, there were no bird like sounding whistles. Maybe he was thinking the same as me.

That evening, as I was doing my homework, I heard a continuous bird like whistling, coming from our back garden, that backed on to our bedroom. I was so nervous, in case my sisters or my parents heard them. I knew it was Firoz. He could not have come into the garden itself, as it was all fenced with a thick hedge, though, there were a few gaps, here and there. The whistling soon stopped.

Once again, the next afternoon, Firoz did not walk with me. I had a note for him. It would have to wait till I next saw him.

Another day passed, another day, he didn't walk with me. In one way I was heartbroken, and other, I was pleased that it had ended, as I was risking too much, seeing him.

That evening, when it had gone dark, I heard the bird whistles again. My parents were in the sitting room. On the other side of the house, past their bedroom, and the dining room. My sisters were out of the room, and I was doing my homework. Would anyone notice, if I just slipped out in the back garden, to hand over the note to Firoz? I suddenly plucked up courage and went out through the bathroom, into the back garden, the note in my hand. The whistles got softer in tone. He must have seen me coming out even though it was pitch dark in the garden. I went towards the hedge, where I could hear him, and I could see a red dot of flame glowing, on and off. Which I later found was a cigarette. He was on the outside of the hedge, I handed him the note, he took it, and placed one in my hand. We whispered, hello and good bye, and I ran home, before I was missed by my family.

I read his note again and again. I smelt it, it smelt of cigarette and the scent of cologne. Then placed it between the sleeves of a book. That's where all the notes would be kept.

These meetings went on for a few weeks. We wouldn't do our walk anymore, but I would run out into the back garden, whenever the coast was clear, and when I heard the birds whistling. Exchanging notes that had loving lyrics from the latest songs.

There would be times, when it was not safe to slip out of the back door, so I would just listen to the bird like whistling till it finally faded and then stopped.

It was a lovely relationship we had. I felt liked and loved, even though it was not the kind of love, I had seen in the

Bollywood movies. I had also learned from the movies that, what we were doing would never be approved by my family, even if it was merely exchanging some notes.

If we were ever caught talking to each other, I would be punished and grounded for bringing shame to the family.

I was in my last year of Secondary education. The navy blue colour on my school skirt, was fading, bleached by the sun. Also, my shoes were wearing away, but I was afraid to mention this to my mum.

My dad had to send money over to my brothers in England, so there were lots of cut downs in the expenses. I decided to take every stitch apart of the skirt, turned every piece of material inside out, as it was still dark blue on the reverse side, and sew it all back. I ended up with an almost new skirt.

My friend Ranjeet was happy for me to have an old pair of shoes from her collection. So, we walked to her house one lunch break, and I tried out her shoes. They were slightly big on me, but I stuffed a bit of cotton wool in them, and they fitted perfectly.

We were always afraid to ask for new bras or underwear from my mum, so we would wash and wear the few that we had, as often as we could. Till she bought us new ones.

The end of term exams were over, and I was supposed to go to my school to collect my results. I was heading off to school when I bumped into Firoz. He was with a friend. He told me that he had a day off, and was just killing time with his friend. They walked with me to my bus, but on the way, Firoz kept suggesting that they would come to my school with me, as there would be no classes for me. I was very nervous about them coming to my school, but they hopped on the bus with me, and suggested that they would be discreet, and keep away from me, so that my friends would not know that they were there with me.

We reached my school and walked through the school gates. They were admiring my school and said that I was lucky to be studying in such a wonderful school.

We walked to the class, where the list of results would be printed on sheets of paper, displayed on the notice board.

I didn't come across any of my friends, so we went closer to the notice board. There it was, my name on the list. Out of seven subjects, I had only passed in two. The rest was all 'fails'.

Upon seeing this Firoz was in a shock. He said that he always believed that I was a very clever girl and would have done better than I had. I was very embarrassed, especially when Firoz's friend had been there too.

I just cannot forget the expression on Firoz's face after seeing my results.

Little did he know that, when in primary school, on our way home in his car, my dad would look at my sister's and my results and would repeat 'Maya failed, Binder failed' all the way home.

My dad being a teacher, and knowing the right people in the right places, and just by being in a high standard school, did not change anything for us. We were still very bad at our studies.

Firoz and his friend decided to leave, so that I could find and mingle with my friends. I was glad that none of my friends had seen me with Firoz and his friend. My secret was safe.

Once we had gone to the Drive-in Cinema with our parents. We were sat in the back seat, waiting for the film to start. Most youngsters would form groups and walk up and down, between the rows of cars, just walking and meeting up with friends.

I suddenly noticed that, a couple of blokes passed in front of our car. One of them was Firoz. He was busy chatting away to his friend. I got so excited that he was going to be watching the same film as me.

We had a great relationship. A beautiful friendship. I was a happier person since I met him. It was very hard though, that I couldn't share my happiness with any of my friends or family members.

I was a young teenager, going through emotions, and not thinking of the consequences or the outcome of this relationship. Just like having a crush on a teacher gets you nowhere.

One day, I had been to the shops, to run errands for my mum. On my way home, I bumped into Firoz. He started walking with me, and asked me, if I would like to see where he lived. I agreed, even though I thought, it was a bit risky.

When we got to where he lived I realised that he only lived few hundred yards from our house, opposite the main road. He walked me into a 'Skati'. A 'Skati' was a courtyard with lots of rooms, in all four directions. There would be different families living in these rooms, may be a couple of rooms each per family and a little kitchen. They would share the water tap, and perhaps the bathroom which was a wet room and toilets.

I walked into his room, where a Boy was doing some ironing. I sat on a chair, and he said that he would bring me a cup of tea. I looked around the room, while he was gone. There was a double bed in the room, a small table, with a radio on it. Two chairs, one of which I was sitting on. A very basic room, with hardly any furniture. There was no wardrobe, and the clothes hung on hooks on the wall, and some hanging from hooks behind the door. The Boy kept glancing at me with a smile, as he carried on with the ironing. Firoz returned with two cups of tea, placed on saucers, rattling as he placed one in my hand.

An elderly woman followed him. She had a long floral dress on, and her grey hair was in a bun.

He introduced me to her, as his mother. They spoke in their tongue that I couldn't understand. She smiled at me and spoke words I couldn't understand, and then she disappeared.

He sat on the bed and we both sipped on our tea. We chatted, and then suddenly he said that this is the life he wanted to give me, with a servant to do the house work, and his mother look after me. And that I would not have to lift a finger.

I was surprised to hear all that. I blushed and went all hot and tingly. Words wouldn't come out of my mouth. This handsome young man wanted to care for me. Did he really think that we could live together? Was this ever going to be possible? Did Firoz live in a dream land?

Even I knew in my heart that this was never going to be possible in a million years.

My parents would rather see me dead then let me go ahead with this fairy-tale kind of existence. I made my excuses and announced that I had to leave, in case I got into trouble, from being late home.

He walked me out of the Skati, and I ran home.

That night, I thought about Firoz. There were loads of doubts going on in my mind. Like, was he expecting me to live with him, from what he had said, or was he just saying that in jest?

Trouble was, that we hardly ever talked. We had never talked about our families. All we ever did was hand over notes to each other, with lyrics from romantic songs.

I also wondered if he thought that I came from a very wealthy family. For we did live in a large bungalow. Surrounded with beautiful gardens. And because I lived in a big house, would that have been the reason he thought that I would have also been good in my studies, and not failed in most subjects?

He lived in a Skati that his family shared with other families. Despite these feelings, and having doubts, no way was I prepared to end this beautiful relationship, and friendship. There wasn't a single day that I didn't miss him. Couldn't wait to hand him my note, and receive one from him, smelling of perfume and cigarettes, that would be read over and over again, then secretly placed in the sleeves of a book.

These feelings made me a bit careless at times. If ever he was to pass near my house in the day time, and if I was to notice him, I would run out to talk to him. There was a gap, between our garage and the fence that divided our house with our neighbour, Mr Patel.

I would run there, and have a chat with him, even if it was for few minutes.

My carelessness got me into trouble one day.

My dad had been having a walk with Mr Patel, after dinner, which they did most late afternoons. When he returned from his walk, I was with my sister in our bedroom, doing our studies, then my mum called my name out, and asked me to go to the sitting room. As I walked in, my dad was sat on the sofa, and my mum went and sat next to him. My head went all hot, and I felt a bit faint, when my dad said that Mr Patel reckons, that I had been seen chatting to a man, and asked me if it was true. Words wouldn't come out of my mouth, and I had to think fast. I blurted out, that yes, I did, but he was a friend's brother, and I was just asking about her. My parents warned me to be careful, and not ever talk to men, or boys, or else I would be in a lot of trouble. I promised that I wouldn't and went and joined my sisters, tears running down my cheeks.

That night I sobbed under my covers, and couldn't see how I was going to avoid Firoz. Will I never be able to see him and talk to him ever again? And exchange notes?

The next day I decided to go to Firoz's house and warn him, that we had been seen chatting, and that we would have to stop seeing each other. I left a little early for school, so I could do that. I had a beige Mac on, that my dad had brought for us from England on his recent visit.

I was just about to cross the road, when I noticed my dad's car turning from our home towards the main road on the way to his school. I quickly turned around and disappeared in the road, by the Mosque.

I didn't know at that time, if he had seen me. For not many young girls wore Mac's in a hot country like Uganda. Especially one identical to the one he himself had brought over from England. Had my dad seen me, and recognised me?

I took the bus to school as usual. I just couldn't concentrate on anything that day. I had to get a message to Firoz, to warn him, and may be ask him to shave his moustache and goatee off so our neighbour did not recognise him, if ever seen again, and point him out to my Dad.

So, I wrote him a long note. The next time, I heard the bird like whistle, and I was able to slip out of the house, I gave him the note and also told him that we had to be very careful from now on. I also mentioned about him shaving off his moustache and goatee.

Our meetings in the garden stopped, and we would only be able to chat, if we were to bump into each other, away from prying eyes.

Of course, he did not shave off his face!

Soon as our relationship had started, it ended, just in three months of seeing each other.

While walking back home from school one day, as I almost approached my house, a lady walked towards me and started shouting at me. Waving her finger at me, she demanded that I stop messing with her brother's life. She said I was too young for him and was stopping him from finding and settling with the right girl.

I didn't know where to put my face. I didn't utter a single word. I was speechless. I was hoping that none of our neighbours had heard, or seen what had just happened. I turned towards our home, when she walked away, still muttering something. She was very angry. She was Firoz's sister.

I was so heart broken, and was scared too, in case Firoz's family members knocked at our door, and warned my parents about us. Then they would know that I had lied to them, when I had been confronted, just weeks ago.

My world had shattered, I felt lonely, and not being able to talk to anyone about the pain I was going through. At the age of fifteen, ignorant and innocent about life, I was carrying such a burden alone.

His family must have found out about us, from his mother. She must have told them about the time when I had gone over to his house to see him. His family must have had a word with him, like my parents had done with me, perhaps, he too wasn't able to stay away from me. So, his sister was sent to warn me.

The bird like whistling stopped, the notes stopped, the little chats, whilst bumping into each other stopped. My whole world had stopped.

There was nothing I could have done. After all the relationship we had had could never carry on forever. I was too young and he was an older man. We were of different religion. It had just been like a dream, and all dreams come to an end at some point.

I would read over and over, the notes I had saved. I would either have a good cry, or smile at the lyrics of the songs he had written. Soon the smell of his cologne and his cigarette scent faded away from his notes, as if a whoosh of wind had suddenly blown them away.

Time just went on, and I tried to put the whole experience to the back of my mind.

Sometimes I would stroll in our garden, hoping to have a glance at Firoz, walking to the Mosque.

A few times I did see him, with his friends, smartly dressed, walking towards the Mosque, busy having a conversation. Not even glancing towards our house.

He had forgotten me.

The 1971 Coup

I was just turning sixteen, and was to finish my senior school, when suddenly there was an upheaval in Uganda. Dr Milton Abote was the President of Uganda at that time. He was planning to arrest Idi Amin for misappropriating army funds.

Idi Amin was with the King's African Rifles, of the British Colonial Army. He had started off as a cook. But then he rose to the rank of a Lieutenant.

When Uganda gained Independence from the United Kingdom, in 1962, Idi Amin remained in the Armed forces. He reached the rank of a Major, and was appointed Commander of the Uganda Army in 1965.

Before he could be arrested, in 1971, he launched a military coup and thus declared himself the president.

Soon there was a presence of military jeeps and soldiers all over Kampala city.

We had a good view of the Kampala Road from our house. We would see military jeeps travelling up hill, towards the Kabaka's Palace. That had become Idi Amin's base.

Kabaka's Palace, otherwise known as the Royal home of Buganda, was in Mungo which was a suburb of Kampala.

He ordered execution of a mass number of Lango and Acholi Christian tribes, who had been loyal to Abote. Whoever opposed his regime was terrorised and killed. He became a dictator.

In early 1972, Idi Amin ordered expulsion of up to at least seventy thousand Asians, giving them ninety days to leave the country with limited amount of cash and belongings.

Uganda was in a chaos. And people were panicking. Our parents stopped us from going to school, in fear that we could be harmed, or even killed.

My father soon started making arrangements for fleeing the country. My mum started packing clothes and her favourite kitchenware that she had used since she had left India and brought along with her, in large wooden chests that my father had ordered. As this would be the maximum allowance, to be taken out of Uganda.

The large chests would be sent separately, not too sure if by cargo boats or planes.

We couldn't even sell any of our furniture or household belongings, as we were only allowed to leave with a set amount of money per family, and a suitcase each per person. All our belongings and furniture were left just as they were. We were aware that our house would have been looted or occupied by the locals, as soon as we were to leave.

There were families that were too poor to find money for their fares.

So, the people who were well to do were helping them out. Some of the elderly people were illiterate, so were being helped by friends, with filling forms and buying tickets for their fare.

One family, that was really helpful was, my old friend Suda, from my Arya Samaj School. Her family had businesses all over Kampala.

They offered money with any other help, to people who needed it. And I learned that my friend Nirmala's family were helped by them too.

My father made a bonfire, on one side of the garden, and burnt piles of letters, he had been receiving from families in India, and from my brothers, and uncles in England. He also burnt some official documents that were no good to him anymore.

We were also burning our school books in the bonfire. We felt so sad, seeing years of memories, turn into ashes.

Along with my books, I let all my notes from Firoz burn in the fire, and see them turning into charred pages. Each line of beautiful lyrics disappearing before my teary eyes, till there were no more.

I felt like I had thrown all my beautiful memories on to a pyre. It would have been too risky to carry them with me, to England, for I had heard that the Customs at Entebbe Airport were searching every bit of people's luggage, along with doing body searches.

My dad was busy making last minute arrangements for our passports. Most of the families were going back to the countries they had originally come from, like India and Pakistan. Or whatever country was prepared to give them sanctuary.

As my dad had come to Uganda during the British Rule, he was able to immigrate to England. He alerted my brothers and uncles, that we would be leaving Uganda as soon as the passports and the required documents were ready.

We were watching the news on the television, of the people arriving in different parts of England, and put into camps.

Majority of the Asians were placed in the camps in the RAF base at The Greenham Common in Newbury, some families ended up in Leicester, and around London.

My dad was worried, as he didn't wish to have his wife and three young girls living in the camps.

He was very stressed and concerned about our future.

He gave his precious car to one of the African staff members from his school. He also let Tommy be taken by him as he had a little house with a bit of land, where he used to grow coffee. He had little kids too. So, Tommy would fit in nicely in his family.

I remember our dad taking us to his house, during Diwali times, when we would take offerings of sweetmeats to his humble home. He had little kids, who would run around us, almost naked.

He had a little shamba, outside of his house, where he would grow coffee, cassava and other crops, in order to feed his family. After each visit of ours to his shamba, he would give us a bag full of roasted coffee beans to take with us.

Before my dad had given his car away, there was a frightening incident, where my dad was just about to drive out of our garage, when a local man, armed with a Panga, a machete kind of knife tried to pull my father out of the car in order to steal it. Luckily a neighbour's son happened to be passing by, and came to my father's rescue, and chased the thief away.

Both my father and the young lad were very lucky, that they didn't get hurt or killed.

It was a miracle, as the young lad, only had one arm. One of his arms had been amputated from below his elbow, due to some disease in his childhood. He lived four doors away from our house. He was the son of the neighbours, just a few doors away, and good friends of our parents and were both teachers.

This incident made my father more determined to leave Kampala as soon as possible. It was getting a bit scary, to live amongst looters and killers. There were rumours that some young women had also been raped by the soldiers. The law was getting out of hand too. None of these killers and looters were punished, as Idi Amin's Army encouraged the locals to scare the Asians out of their country.

Our Journey to England.

In the end of September 1972, we boarded a plane to leave the beautiful country, where I had spent my sixteen years, for good, to a country, with a different culture and weather. We used to hear stories from friends of the family, who had been to England that it snowed heavily in the winter. There were four seasons - spring summer, autumn and winter. Uganda had the same season all year round, apart from some rainy seasons. They also talked about couples with small children who would do separate shifts, in order to have one parent at least looking after the kids. Sometimes they hardly saw each other, till the weekend or holidays.

Most of the women, who would have been housewives, while their husbands went out to work or run businesses, who had come from India or Africa would have to work in factories or in jobs they were able to do, in order to run the house. No longer was one pay enough

It was the first time for me and my sisters to fly on a plane. My parents had already been to England previously. So, we were very excited, when we boarded the plane at Entebbe Airport, where previously we had waved goodbye to our brothers, when they left for England.

We had gone through Customs, where every corner of our luggage was scanned, not with scanners, but by the naked eyes of the strict Custom officers, making sure that we were not hiding forbidden items, amongst our clothing.

Our mum had loaded our wrists with gold bangles, and chains around our necks, in order to be able to take at least some of her gold out of the country, by distributing it amongst her daughters, hoping that it would not be confiscated. We were very lucky that nothing was confiscated, as Maya and I were old enough to be wearing jewellery.

Most of the Ugandan Asians fled the land they had called home for years. All the families we knew of had either already left or had just days left to leave.

We land in England

We landed at Heathrow Airport. All the surroundings looked strange. The airport looked so clean. Very different to the Entebbe Airport, which was basic, where you would simply enter the main doors, wait in the checking-in lounge and simply show your passports, and then out of the Departure doors. Then just walk straight onto the tarmac, and board our plane.

But Heathrow Airport was vast, and once we left the plane, we had a very long walk through tunnels till we reached the Customs, and then again a long walk till we got to baggage Collection point. It was very exciting for us, to see so many people, going about their business, in an organised manner.

We were welcomed by our brothers and other family members, who had come to receive us.

There was a different smell, all around us, to the smell of Africa. It was the month of October, so there was the autumn chill in the air. It smelt like our uncle's cold storage in Nairobi.

The drive from the airport to our destinations was very short, as most of our family lived very near to the airport.

We were kindly put up by our widowed aunt, in her three-bedroom house. She accommodated us all, despite having two young children, by making extra bedding, and us sharing beds. My aunt's kindness and support meant that we were lucky, not to end up in the camps.

My aunt's parents, lived just a few doors away on the same road as her. We would be invited there for dinner most days.

My brother, Gulab, had got engaged to my aunt's sister Madhu previously, so we were one large family, especially as we had been familiar with the family, when in Kampala.

We soon adapted to the different way of life. Madhu's younger sister Bina would take us to different agencies to register for job finding. And also introduced us to different shops like C &A for clothes, Boots for toiletries and makeup and Woolworths for day to day needs. We found it very strange the first time we were taken to Woolworth by Bina. We noticed her picking various goods and placing them in a basket, but were relieved when she took the basket full of goods to the till and paid for them. This would not have been allowed in Uganda, where the goods would be handled by the shopkeeper and handed over to the customer after payment was made.

My Didi and I didn't have good enough grades to go into college, so our only option was to find work whereas Rakish continued her studies in a local school.

We found a job at a car component manufacturing factory, called Magnatex which was not far from where we lived. We would walk to work, and do eight-hour shifts.

I was put on a line that assembled car lamps, and Didi on assembling cigarette lighters, and she was to work solo. We worked on piece work and had to work very fast and hard in order to reach our given target of completing a given amount of pallets to fill per shift. It was so exciting to get our pay packet, at the end of each week, and feel grownup enough to be earning money.

It was a bit exciting to be working, and not having to go to school. It felt good having that freedom that we didn't have in Uganda.

My dad found work at the airport working for Air Canada. And my mum at Trust House Forte, which was a catering company.

Previously he had been offered a job at a school for disabled and special needs children, but he didn't think that he had the capability to fulfil that job. Then he got a job at a building site, but that job did not suit him either. The Air Canada job was to be the one for him.

Soon my brother Gulab and Ashok put together their savings, borrowed some money and managed to have enough to put a deposit down on a house.

The house they found was on the same street as my aunt's, who lived at No 104, their mum's family at No 59 and we had moved into No 81, on the same street. This brought all our families very close, and we would be in and out of each other's houses, exchanging food.

In December, Gulab got married to Madhu, so she too moved in with us. We all somehow managed with the sleeping arrangements, sharing beds. Also sharing one bathroom and toilet.

I don't recall a single day when anyone of us complained about lack of facilities. Our daily routine ran smoothly.

During the cold evenings, after dinner, we would all gather in the backroom, which was the only room with a coal fire, and chat amongst ourselves, till it was time for bed.

It was much better than having to share with strangers in the camps, if we had ended up there, we thought.

The house had previously been rented out to some Hippies and students. The colours they had chosen to paint on the walls were very bright, so all the rooms had to be repainted.

There was a large shed at the back of the house which was full of old furniture, bric-a-brac and boxes and bags full of clothes.

We used some of the good stuff, and got rid of most of the rubbish.

My sisters and I went through the clothes and picked some of the better quality ones, for ourselves.

I started wearing these western clothes, and felt good in them. I also starting wearing mini dresses and bellbottoms which was the fashion then.

Our new-found freedom meant that we were allowed to wear western clothes. Our parents never stopped us from doing so. In fact, I was in a mini skirt once, with tights and boots up to my knees. My dad commented that I looked like one of the girls from Abba.

I would go into Boots and pick some makeup. I took a liking to Mary Quant Products. I would wear dark lipstick and have dark eye makeup, which looked very gothic. That became my style and look for some years.

We were invited to loads of parties, at Madhu's mum's place. We would dance to the latest music that was played on the Top of The Pops. We soon got familiar with the English music, and English and American Bands. Yet we also danced to some of the Bollywood music and often danced to Bhangra music. We would cook loads of food and have a feast. We didn't need any outsiders, we had enough family members to throw a party.

I got very fond of the English music, my favourite being Abba, Elvis, Michel Jackson and Parry Como.

Ashok and Bina got married in July 1974. They moved into No 81 too. They would take me and my sisters to funfairs, and parks at weekends, and we soon got accustomed to the life in England.

Gulab and Madhu had their first child. A beautiful girl, whom they named Sharon.

I used to love taking pictures of her, with my new camera. Since she was the first grandchild and our first niece, everyone doted on her. Especially my dad.

I would accompany Madhu, when she took Sharon out in her pram, for a walk.

We would watch English programmes of the Seventies, like Love thy Neighbour, Please Sir, and various other sitcoms.

I also loved watching Bette Davis movies, and the Westerns.

Didi and I made loads of new friends at work. We would all gather at lunch times and share our food. There was a young Gujarati Girl who happened to be going out with an English bloke. Once she was chatting to him and I heard him say that he will not be able to see her that night as he would be working behind the bar. I could not understand what he meant by that. Why would he be working behind a bar? I thought that he was going to be working behind a bar, as in a building. It took us ages to follow the English language, spoken by the British. The English spoken in Uganda was basic.

I recall the time when I was having my break, in the factory yard, when I saw Norman Wisdom walking along with one of the office staff. I was very excited to see an actor from the television programme I loved watching.

My Didi was almost in her early twenties, so a marriage was arranged for her. The young man had come over to England from India, to his sister's place and they were looking for a suitable match for him. As per custom in those days, a middle man, in this case a middle woman, tried to arrange the marriage between Didi and the young man. When both the parties were happy with the arrangement, all the formalities took place and the marriage went ahead.

Didi was the most beautiful bride in the world. She looked radiant in her wedding outfit. She looked like the Bollywood actresses we used to admire on the movie screens. After the wedding ceremony, she came back to our house, only to be taken away by her husband. This was usually the ceremony where the bride was carried in a wooden carriage with handles on both sides, decorated with flowers, called Doli. This would be held by two men, one on each end. But in the modern times, cars are used for this purpose.

When Didi walked to the Doli (The car that was decorated with flowers and a red ribbon to symbolise a wedding car) we all followed her, and there wasn't a single dry eye. That was the first time in my entire life, I had seen my dad wail. His precious daughter was leaving for good. My precious sister, who had been my soul mate, and a soulmate to Rakish would start her life with a stranger, and a new family.

We missed Didi a lot, but then it got easier, as she would often come and visit us with my brother-in-law.

My Didi and my brother-in-law soon bought their own property, and settled down only few miles' distance from us.

Trying to better myself

I found that the local school was to hold evening classes for beginners in French. I decided to enrol myself, for I had studied a bit of French in my secondary school, and wanted to polish up on it.

Since the course started in September, I would have to walk to and from the school in the dark.

One of my fellow students, an elderly man, I would guess in his sixties, offered to give me a lift back home after the lessons, as he lived next street to ours. He would drop me to my door.

My dad was not happy about this arrangement, so he would walk to the school and wait for us to come out after the classes ended, then jump in the car with me. I guess, being a parent, he was very protective towards his daughters.

I soon gave up my French class, when it was decided that we were to make a trip to France, to learn more about the culture. No way would my dad allow me to do that.

Then I decided to purchase a Linguaphone course, so I could study from home.

This too didn't last long, I was struggling to follow it through.

I was missing my sister, at the factory. Some of the ladies whom I worked with, encouraged me to find a job in an office, rather than work in a factory at my age. I took their advice and joined a job finding agency. Soon I had about four interviews to go to. The first one went okay, it was for a stock control clerk for a small firm. But the second job sounded promising. It was to be for a filing clerk for BOC (British Oxygen Company). I was happy to join this company, and didn't even bother to go to the next two job interviews. I soon gave in my notice at Magnatex and started my new job in Brentford, Middlesex. I was to work in an open plan office with six sales people. My job was to file large files containing Computer sheets and keep the filing up to date. My boss Mr Tom Morrish was kind and helpful, and showed me the ropes. The staff were nice to me too. To begin with, I was very nervous, but soon settled into my job. I was introduced to a new manager, a Mr James Cockburn. He was the coordinator for welding products. Soon I had to do his filing too. My job also consisted of posting leaflets and catalogues of our products to the companies that requested them and was also in charge of ordering stationery, and supply to the office workers.

When sending off leaflets to customers, the addresses would be handwritten in ink.

Soon Mr Morrish provided me with an electric Golfball typewriter so that I could make them look more professional. I was also encouraged to type a few short memos for my senior colleagues. Normally these would have been sent to the typing pool, and there was no guarantee how soon they would be typed and sent back to our office. I was very slow. I couldn't touch type. But managed somehow.

Mr Morrish was very happy with my progression. He decided to send me on a Typing course, at a local Isleworth polytechnic, once a week. I still didn't master touch typing but managed to learn a few new skills.

At lunch times, I would sit at my desk, and have a cup of tea and a crusty cheese bun bought from the tea lady who would came along with her trolley of newspapers, magazines and snacks. I would pass my lunchtimes reading books by James Hadley Chase, the writer of great thrillers. Rest of the staff would go down to the canteen or the local pub for lunch. I was too shy to mingle in with them in that way.

One day, I was encouraged to go to the local pub with the staff members. With some persuasion I did end up going with them.

There were about seven of us, three ladies and four men. We walked into a very traditional looking pub, across the road from our office building. It was full of a lunch time crowd, and was very noisy. One of my managers, My Perry, asked me, what I would like to drink, I didn't hesitate and said, 'Coke, please!

'Come on, have a proper drink'! he said. I had no idea about drinks, so I said the first thing that came to me, 'Martini please'! The only drink I was familiar with due to having seen it in the James Bond films.

I tasted the martini. It was a bitter taste, so I just sipped on it, till it was time to leave.

The second time I ever had an alcoholic drink was on our Works Christmas party. We sat at beautifully laid tables in our canteen. The food was served by waiters. I felt so grown up, eating with my bosses and colleagues. I would watch to see what knives and forks were being used by the people next to me, before I started, in case I ate with the wrong cutlery. The guy next to me poured me a glass of wine. I had a sip of it every now and then, and didn't seem to mind the taste of it.

After dinner, every one spread around chatting to each other. I didn't know what to do, so I went and stood against the wall, watching everyone. Then my boss, James Cockburn walked up to me and handed me a glass of wine. He must have noticed, that I was feeling nervous, and was not good with mingling with the crowd. He held a conversation with me, while I sipped on the wine. Soon I found that my legs were giving way and I could hardly stand, without the help of the wall. James Cockburn noticed this, and advised me that I have no more wine. I have no idea, how I got home that day. All I know is that I had taken at least two buses to get home. I wondered if my family had noticed that I had been drinking.

I settled into my job at B.O.C very nicely. My boss, Mr Morris, would call me into his office, and announce that I had progressed so well, so should be getting a pay rise. That would make my day and encourage me to do even better. My boss, Mr Cockburn, was always very inquisitive to listen to me about my life in Africa and my journey to England. He would also try and correct my pronunciation, of words I said wrong. Somehow, he felt like bettering me, and teaching me things I was not aware of about the English culture. It was like he was trying to nurture me with knowledge. I now think that he was the one who encouraged Mr Morris to send me on a typing course, and providing me with a new electric typewriter.

We became very good friends, despite the age difference, as I was just turning twenty one, and he was a grey haired man, about my dad's age, perhaps in his mid-fifties. He would call me on my internal phone line, asking me to take some files to his office. I would do so, and then he would chat to me, like he wasn't my senior, and that he wasn't my boss.

My colleagues sussed out that, his calls for requesting me to take files over were just an excuse. Sometimes James Cockburn would walk into our open plan office humming POM! POM! POM! POM!

He would greet everyone and talk business with his juniors with them calling him 'Sir'.

He was an important figure in our company, respected by all, and yet when we had our chats, I was never made to feel inadequate.

I used to travel to work on the buses. So, I decided to take up driving lessons. My dad asked the driving instructor, who had given him lessons previously, to teach me to drive.

It was very nerve wracking to begin with, but the instructor kept control of the car with the dual controls, if ever I went out of control.

After numerous lessons, he put me down for a test. Unfortunately, I failed my first test, then the second, and the third.

I decided to change my instructor after that, as I felt that he was not really correcting my mistakes, but just letting me drive around.

He once stopped at West Middlesex Hospital, during my lesson, and asked me to wait in the car, while he went and saw his elderly mother, who was in a ward, at this hospital. I waited for at least half an hour. When he returned, he asked me if I could go with him to see his mum, as she did not believe him, when he said that he had a learner waiting in the car. So, I had to follow him to the ward to say hello to his mum, just so that she believed that he was not making excuses.

I soon stopped having lessons from him, and started searching for another instructor.

I began my lessons with a new instructor, and found that he was correcting my mistakes, and taught me a lot more than the old instructor. I applied for a test, when I felt confident enough with my driving.

I thought that I was doing very well on my test, then I made one little mistake, and noticed the examiner jotting something on the form on his clipboard. My nerves set in, and my legs began shaking. My head just went, and I got very nervous. Unfortunately, I failed my test yet again.

This was getting a bit embarrassing for me by now, as I would announce it to my family and my colleagues about my test, then had to tell them that I had failed.

My work mates, would watch me from the windows of the seventh floor of the building, where our office was situated, drive away in my instructor's car, to have my test. Then return to announce that I had failed. I would get their sympathy, along with wishing me, 'better luck next time'!

How many times had I heard that before, but luck was never on my side.

My lessons continued, and then it was time for yet another test. On the day of my test, I had been feeling unwell with flu like symptoms. I was thinking of ringing up and cancelling my test. But then changed my mind. I went to the cupboard, where my dad had placed miniature bottles of brandy that he used to end up bringing from Air Canada. I drank the whole bottle in one go. We often used this for medicinal purposes.

I went for my one hour lesson, before the test, and my instructor said that I had a great chance of passing, after my performance that day. I went off for my test, feeling very rough, and full of cold and a heavy chest. I didn't care if I passed or failed, as I drove around, on the instructions of the Examiner. I stopped the car, when we reached the Test Centre. I was asked some theory questions, which I answered with confidence as I had practised them so many times previously. The examiner turned around and said the most precious words, 'Miss Sharma, congratulations, you have passed!'

I could not contain myself upon hearing his words. I had done it at last. Passed the fifth time. I think the brandy had calmed my nerves.

My family and my colleagues were very pleased to hear that I had passed my test at last.

I had already bought a car, a triumph Toledo, before I had even passed my test. When I had started my driving lessons, not knowing that it would take me so long to pass my test I had started looking for cars in the local newspapers.

My parents had gone on a trip to India. My dad used to get concession on flights from Air Canada, so he often used to travel to India, to see his family. He had also travelled to Canada, Germany, Singapore and various other countries, with my mum. So, while they were away, I asked my brother Gulab to collect the car for me, which I had paid £100 for. The car would sit in our drive, waiting for me to be able to drive it.

One of my friends, I worked with at Magnatex, had invited me to her Indian wedding. I wanted to go, and I wanted to dress up in one of my mum's sarees. Fit for the occasion.

As my parents were abroad, and Gulab and Madhu had gone out for the day, I needed to get to the wedding. I was too shy to hop on the buses, with a saree on, so I decided to jump into my car, despite having no insurance, tax, or a full driving licence, ended up driving to the wedding.

I was very lucky to be back home in one piece. And not been caught by the police.

When my parents arrived back from India, they brought along a photo of a young man, they were planning me to be married off to.

Apparently, when I was twenty years of age, my parents had started searching for a suitable boy for me. I was shown loads of photos of young men, but nothing came of it. Then one day a couple came to our house, to arrange my marriage with their son. In fact they had come to see if I was a good match for their son. I was asked to join my parents and the guests in the sitting room, so they could, more or less view me, and decide if I was a good match for their son.

While they were there, my Didi and my brother -in -law came over to visit us. They too joined the guests. I was shown a photo of the young man, and he seemed okay. I would not have a say in the matter anyhow. If the two families agreed, I would have to end up marrying him. That was the custom.

When they left, my brother-in-law, suggested that, one of his younger brothers could be a good match for me, and that there was no point in looking for another match.

After a long discussion, it was agreed by both parties that I would marry his younger brother. When my parents arrived from their trip to India, they had been to see my brother-in-law's family, and had agreed to go ahead with the marriage arrangements.

I was shown his photo, and I was happy to go ahead with the marriage plans, just like Didi had been just a few years before that.

Then there were the formalities of arranging for him to come over to England, through immigration.

We would correspond through letters, which we had to do to prove to the officials that we were in a relationship and our marriage was not a plan for him to enter this country. He would write to me in Hindi. My mum would read the letters to me, and then I would reply back, as well as I could, by searching the words I had to write from a Hindi book for beginners as my Hindi reading and writing skills were minimal.

Married Life

Arun arrived in England in December 1976. Arrangements were made, so that my parents and I were to go to my Didi's house, so I could meet him.

He was supposed to ring my brother-in-law from the airport, to be collected, but he ended up hiring a taxi and arrived at their doorstep.

When my parents and I went over, my Didi asked me to go and meet him in their garden where he would be waiting for me.

My first thought, upon seeing him was, Oh my God!!! He is a giant of a man, over six feet and heavily built compared to my five feet, four inches, and a mere seven stones in weight.

I noticed his big hands as he shook hands with me. He was talking to me, but I seemed to be in a daze, and didn't catch what he was saying. His way of talking was different to mine, he spoke very fast and loud whereas I often spoke softly.

We went into the house, and my Didi asked me if I was happy to go ahead.

It was too late now, I thought to myself. I didn't want to disappoint my parents or my Didi and brother-in-law, and nodded, to indicate that I was.

We were betrothed, and the wedding plans were being made.

As we were family, my brother-in-law did not press my family for a big dowry which was customary in Indian weddings.

I had been buying new clothes of my choice, and been storing them in my bottom drawer. My mum had bought me some sarees and other items to take with me. I had also saved a good amount of money in my building society from my earnings, to take with me too.

She had also bought me two sets of gold necklaces with matching earrings, and some gold bangles.

Arun and I got married in a Registry Office in Brentford on 11th March 1977. Some of my work colleagues as well as my boss, Tom Morrish, attended my marriage ceremony. Tracy, who worked in our office offered to be my bridesmaid.

We had a professional photographer hired for the wedding photos.

The court marriage went okay.

This was to be followed by an Indian wedding a few months later. I was to stay with my parents, till the Indian ceremony had taken place.

My Didi would chaperone us, if we were to meet. She took us to the City of London to go sightseeing.

Arun would ring me at my work place sometimes. His English was not very good, so my Didi would write down, on a piece of paper the words, to ask for me, when the receptionist answered the phone. She would transfer the call to my internal line. I used to get so embarrassed talking to him as all my colleagues could hear me in our open plan office. I always tried to make the conversation as short as possible.

Saying that, he soon started buying newspapers. He would try and better his English and knowledge of the new country he had just arrived in.

My boss, James Cockburn, would always talk me out of getting married to a man I had not even seen or known. He couldn't digest the tradition and our way of arranging marriages.

He was worried that one day I might regret going through with it. He was like a father figure to me, and thus worried about what I was putting myself through. But despite his wise advice, I still went along with the arranged marriage. And soon gave in my notice at B.O.C before I had my traditional Indian wedding.

The Indian wedding was low key. Only a few friends were invited, the rest were just family members. I didn't even have a wedding album this time, the only few photos taken were by family members on their little cameras.

After the wedding, I stepped into my Didi's house, not as a sister, but as a daughter-in-law. At least, these were her first words, as I stepped into her threshold, after the Doli ceremony.

We were sent to the Isle of White, to a place called Shanklin, on our honeymoon.

We stayed in a lovely Bed and Breakfast, and had a great time exploring the Island and spending time at the sea side.

Then suddenly, out of the blue, one evening Arun got angry with me over something and began punching and slapping me. I got so scared of his behaviour that I ran out of the hotel and sat against some rocks, on the beach, trying to figure out what had just happened.

It started getting dark, so I had to head back, not knowing what was awaiting me.

He apologised, and we made peace. We had hired a car, and were able to drive around in it, exploring the beautiful Island.

After the honeymoon was over, we had to decide what to do, as a job, as I had already left B.O.C.

Arun found a job at the same factory where my brother-in-law worked. My Didi had a job as well, so I decided to look for work. I did some Temping jobs, each of which would only last a week or two. Then I found a job in a factory that made medical lamps, called Hanovia Lamps.

My job was drilling, which I soon picked up. But soon I discovered that I was pregnant. I stopped working again, before my baby was born. When I announced it to Didi of my pregnancy, she said, that she too was pregnant. So, we were both carrying our babies, more and less at the same time.

I got so emotional, the day I had gone for my antenatal class, and the doctor asked me to pack a bag and make my way to the hospital to be induced.

I was travelling home on the bus, and couldn't stop shaking, tears in my eyes. I was terrified of giving birth, as I didn't know what to expect. After I was induced, I went through long hours of painful labour.

I gave birth to my daughter, Sonal, on 2nd February 1979, at the Canadian Red Cross Hospital in Taplow.

I stayed in hospital for a week, as my blood pressure was very high, and the doctors were not happy to discharge me till they managed to bring it down.

Arun and my family would come to visit me once a day, then in the evening, I would spend time with my new-born.

During the night time, the nurses would bundle up the babies in their hospital cots, and wheel them into the nursery so that the new mums could have a rest and a good sleep.

I loved every minute of my stay in the hospital and had no desire to return home.

This was the first time in my life, I had spent time away, on my own, from my parents or family. No one to answer to, but in return get care and unconditional love. And a beautiful baby by my side.

I didn't at all look forward to returning home.

I was welcomed home, with the new bonny baby. My parents came to visit us too and doted on the new born, who was showered with new clothes and gifts.

I loved being a mum to a beautiful baby. Whenever I was to take Sonal in her pram, people would stop and look, and admire her.

In March, My Didi gave birth to a baby girl. She too was a beautiful baby.

We would both push our babies' prams and take them to the park, and chat and compare notes.

We were one big family, the two brothers, married to the two sisters, and now the babies.

Soon we bought a car for the family, from part of the money from my building society book, the rest had been used to have central heating installed, in the shared house.

I was the only one, who had passed the driving test, at that time. So, I would be the one driving everyone around.

My Didi and I were both not working now, due to the birth of our babies, and Arun and my brother-in-law were busy working at the factory.

They would often come home late, as they would join their bosses for drinks after work. This would annoy my Didi and me, as our dinner time would be delayed, and we would not eat till they were home.

My Didi would spend hours preparing some delicious meals. She was an amazing cook. I was not a good cook, so I would help her with chopping vegetables, and other chores in the kitchen. If they were to come home on time, they would settle down to have a few drinks before the dinner was served. They would end up having a bottle of whiskey, between them.

Soon, Arun took a liking to indulging in whisky daily. This soon turned him depending on it. And he started being aggressive, when drunk.

He would be all happy, chatty and giggly whilst drinking, but when he had had more than he should have, he would turn into an angry and unreasonable man, his behaviour would turn aggressive.

I would be walking on egg shells, afraid to say the wrong words. Most of the times.

I had Didi and my brother-in-law protecting me from his behaviour.

Things took a turn one day. As the four of us were watching a late night film on television, the two men were drinking their whisky, Arun getting drunk by the minute.

When the film was over we all got ready for bed. Not long after we had settled in bed, Arun started shouting abuse at me. He often thought that he had had a bad deal, when it came to marrying me. I wasn't as beautiful as my Didi, who was fair and beautiful, whereas I was dark skinned. The shouting turned into him physically hurting me, so I started crying, and let out a few screams.

My Didi and brother-in-law rushed into our bedroom, to see what was going on.

When I told them of my ordeal, Didi told me to sleep in the spare room, and let Arun calm down. Which I gladly did.

Not long after, I had settled in the spare bedroom, Arun walked over to my bed, and demanded that I go back to our bedroom. I refused to go with him, afraid to make any noise, in case I disturbed my Didi and brother-in-law. And the two babies, in their cots.

He picked me up, and laid me on our bed. Luckily, he didn't cause any more commotion.

That is what the problem was with Arun. He had a split personality.

In the morning, my Didi prepared a breakfast tray for me, and brought it up to the spare bedroom. Shocked, that I was not in bed, she opened our bedroom, and found me lying on our bed with Arun.

That just set her off. She accused me of "crying wolf" and still ending up in Arun's arms, after all the drama I had caused the previous night. She accused me of being a drama queen.

I tried to explain to her what had happened that night, and that I didn't want to cause any more commotion, but she didn't want to know.

That morning, when the men had gone to work. Didi would not acknowledge me, or talk to me.

I didn't know what to do, I was so home sick. One minute I was happy go lucky, enjoying a carefree life with my brothers and their wives, with the newly found freedom from my parents. Having a fulfilling job with great prospects, with great colleagues, who loved me and respected me, to a life where I was being unappreciated by my husband, and my childhood friend, my Didi, who wasn't prepared to hear my side of the story. I felt so trapped. I couldn't even enjoy my new born child, like a new mother would, with all the bitterness going around me.

I would join my Didi for lunch, but she would eat her lunch without me.

Then one day, she said that I should buy my own food and not eat what she had cooked.

I went shopping and bought my groceries, and placed them in the larder.

I would wait till she had done her cooking, and then do my cooking.

We were living separate lives in her house.

I would spend most of the day in our bedroom, tending to my baby.

Then one day she asked me to keep my groceries, separate from hers. She said that my food was inviting mice to the larder which I had truly not witnessed.

I gathered all my food and placed it all in a cardboard box in our bedroom.

Arun was being targeted as well. During his sober hours, he actually felt sorry, the way I was being treated, by my own sister.

I couldn't tell my brothers or my parents what I was going through, as I didn't want to hurt them, also wasn't sure if they would believe me.

My life soon turned upside down. I was not loved or believed by my own sister. My husband used me as a punching bag.

The only thing that kept me going was my baby.

By this time Poly had got married, and moved in with her in-laws and my parents had moved into a council flat in Heston.

My brother Ashok and sister-in-law, Bina, had moved to Peterborough, for that's where their work took them. They started their family, and had a daughter and a son.

Time to leave

There was yet another big argument between the two couples, over Arun's drinking. This time, Didi said that she was not going to tolerate his drunken behaviour, and wanted him to leave her house. She also gave me an ultimatum, that if I was to leave with him, she would have nothing to do with me. After treating me the way she did, of course I left with him. He was my husband, and we had a child to bring up. We packed our bags and took whatever we could in our car, and were to return to collect the rest of our belongings.

We ended up going to my parents' flat, as there was nowhere else to go. They put us up for a couple of nights, but it was not practical, as they lived in a one bedroom flat, with a small living room. Hardly practical for four adults and a baby. And the fact that they had to be up early, in order to go to work.

They advised us to go to the council for help, which we did, and were put up in a Shelter home, and put on a waiting list, till a suitable property was found for us.

The Shelter home was very shabby, and the kind of families that had been placed there were very rough looking.

Some of the women would hang around in the corridors, smoking, what smelt like dope, their young kids running up and down the corridors, making noise.

We could not even have a decent bath, as the shared bathroom would have its tub full of clothes that they would leave to soak.

They would be up all night playing loud music, and drinking.

We could not spend time in that Shelter home in the day time, with a little child, with all that was going on, so we would either go to my parents' flat to have a shower, and a decent meal or we would drive around in our car, passing time. Often, we would end up in Brighton. We would spend the whole day hanging around the beach and the promenade, then return to sleep in uncomfortable beds at the Shelter home. We had to endure all this, for a couple of months till the time we were given a flat.

We soon moved into a new one bedroom flat in Langley. It was a three- storey flat, and we were given the second floor flat.

We soon settled in, with furniture given to us by family.

Surprisingly, Arun found a job at the Ford Motor Factory, which was a walking distance from our flat.

Things were going well for us.

Arun had calmed down, since we left my brother-in-law's, and my sister's place, because he had realised what he had made our child and us go through the past few months. Also, he had not got drunk, like he used to as we didn't have any money to buy food, let alone drink.

Now that we were settled in a new place, we decided to collect our belongings from my brother-in-law's and sister's place. Arun arranged a day for him to go and collect our stuff, along with the gold jewellery my parents had given to me in my dowry which was in a deposit safe in their bank.

He managed to collect most of the stuff, but was not given the jewellery.

There was some kind of disagreement between the two brothers, followed by a physical fight.

In this fight, Arun ended up breaking his brother's arm in two places who had to be rushed to hospital, and ended up having pins fixed to his bones.

Luckily for Arun, his brother didn't press charges.

We had to go through the courts to recovery our jewellery, but lost our case, as it was stated that the jewellery that my parents had given me was part of the dowry, so in a sense did not belong to me.

Now that Arun was earning a decent wage at the Ford factory, we had money coming in, and we were settling into our new flat.

Things took a turn, when Arun started drinking again.

There was a local shop, owned by an Asian man, he would buy his bottle of whiskey from. Sometimes he would drink at the shop with this guy, before returning from the shop, then continue drinking at home. He would be drunk most nights and started being aggressive again.

Sometimes, he wouldn't give me money towards food and housekeeping, but most of the time it would all go towards his drinks. The only money I relied on was the child benefit I got. The worst thing happened when he had a fight with someone at his workplace, and was given the sack, due to his aggressive behaviour. Now there was no money coming in, and he would drink in the daytime as well. His life just revolved around drink.

When he was sober, we would have a laugh and a good time, see my family and drop by to see my parents. We would play cards and scrabble, watch movies and listen to music together. We would hire some VHS movie tapes and watch them. He would have fun playing with Sonal. We often went to the cinema in Southall to watch Bollywood movies. Sonal would either fall asleep in my arms in the cinema hall or sit on my lap and watch the movie. She was never any trouble, despite being just a year old.

Arun even managed to pass his driving test, though I suspect that his licence was illegally obtained, for he never had any lessons, let alone go for a test.

We made friends with a neighbour, who was a social worker, and her husband was a doctor. Arun was always polite and charming in their company.

The whisky would turn him into a monster.

I soon decided to look for a job, as there was no money coming in. I found a job in a cold store, working as a stock controller. I could not rely on Arun looking after Sonal, so I found a child minder, not far from my work place. I would drop her before work and collect her on my way home.

I loved working at the cold store. I worked with five other staff members, in an open plan office, keeping stock of goods going in and out of the cold store. There would be lorries delivering frozen food which would be distributed to various supermarkets. It was good to get away from home and mix with, what I would refer to as normal people. As there had been no normalcy in my life, since I got married. I had lost touch with life itself in general. All I had got accustomed to was an abusive husband and poverty, with a child, who did not have a quality of life that I would have wanted for her.

I had lost my confidence and self-esteem. I was so naïve too.

Once I walked over to the loading-bay at work, to hand over some dockets, to the delivery drivers. One of them shouted, "You and I could make music together."

I shyly replied, "I cannot play any musical instruments."

It wasn't till a long time after, I realised what he had really meant.

I was confident enough, that my child was safe with a childminder, and not at home with a father who would either be with his friends, drinking away, or doing so at home.

Arun decided to go back to India, to see his family. We didn't have enough money for the plane ticket, so he looked up on the little ads in the local newspaper for a loan. He managed to borrow some money from a loan shark and ended up going to India.

I quite enjoyed the peace in my life, during his absence. I would drop Sonal at the child minder, and pick her up on the way home from work, and spend quality time with her, relaxed in my mind, knowing that Arun was not around to make our life hell.

The loan shark would knock on our door each week, for the payment for the loan. I would give him the minimum amount that I could afford, and he would jot that down in the little logbook he had given us. The amount borrowed would somehow keep on building up, rather than be cleared.

I used to dread him knocking at our door, as I could hardly make ends meet, on my wage.

When Arun returned from India, he brought a gold chain for me, a gift from my mother-in-law, whom I had never met. He also brought me and Sonal some clothes.

Time just went by, and he had still not found himself a job. We were really struggling with bills and rent, and paying back the loan to the loan shark.

We would have arguments because of this, and this often ended up in a fight. In fact, fighting became a regular thing. There was a time when he came home very late, drunk. He nudged me to get out of bed and feed him, before I had a chance to wake up properly, he started arguing, that I was a bad wife that I was not in any hurry to feed a starving husband. I rushed to the kitchen to warm up his food, shaking with fear. Then I heard him being sick in the toilet. I went to his aid, and noticed food in his vomit, which meant that he had eaten after all.

When he had settled, I took a plate of warmed up food on a tray to him, but he just tipped the tray off my hands and the food went all over the walls and carpet.

Yet this was all my fault, according to him, and started slapping me around. Sonal who was in her cot next to our bed, woke up and started screaming. He ended up slapping her too.

The time came, when Sonal was so scared of him and dare not cry any more.

A number of times, I left him and ended up at my parents', but he would promise that he would stop drinking and behaving badly, and say 'sorry'.

This circle of events went on and on, of me leaving him, then returning after pleas and promises that he would stop drinking.

He played games with me. I would find small bottles of whisky scattered on the grassy area at the back of our flat, just below our window, where he had disposed of them, instead of the bin. I also found small bottles hidden in the cistern.

There was a time, when I had ended up at my parents again. I made up my mind that I was not going to go back, and stayed at my parents' for a couple of weeks.

He kept on ringing them, making his promises again. But I stayed put, and refused to go back, as he was not only hurting me, but my child too.

Then my dad got a call from him, with a slurred speech saying that he had taken an overdose, and was going to kill himself.

My dad rushed my mum and me into his car, and we rushed to our flat, in an emergency. The journey would have taken half an hour.

As we got there, the front door to the flat had been left ajar. As we went in, he was lying on our bed, one leg hanging off the bed, his eyes rolled up and frothing at his mouth. He was playing dead, yet was still breathing. There were painkillers scattered all over the bed and the floor. We called an ambulance, which arrived quite quickly.

The Paramedics examined him and decided to take him to the hospital.

He was put into the ambulance, but as soon it was about to leave, he got up and walked out of the ambulance saying that he was fine and didn't need to go to hospital.

This had just been an attention seeking act. He had simply staged the scene, in order to get me back home.

I was so fed up and tired of enduring life with him.

He had no morals or shame about his behaviour.

He would end up at my mum's and dad's place of work, asking for money. He would say that we had no money for food. So my parents would give him the money, and he would just blow it on his whisky.

Once my parents made a food parcel, and brought it over to ours, worried that we were going hungry. As they arrived, they found Arun sitting on the sofa, with a bottle of whisky and drunk.

This was the first time they had seen him drunk, as at our normal meetings with our parents, he would be sober.

They promised me that they were never going to hand him any more money, as this would simply feed his habit.

He did not take well to that and cut me off from my family, parents and brothers.

My marriage became a controlling relationship, which no matter what I did, I could not escape.

He didn't love me at all and yet wanted me there to have control over.

He would be watching the television with Sonal, and when a pretty lady appeared on the screen, he would say to her that he was going to get rid of me and get her a new mummy, like the one on the television.

My parents would ring me to make sure that I was okay. I would tell them that he was still up to no good, and took all my weekly earnings from me. In fact, it got to a stage where he would end up coming over to my work place every Friday afternoon, the day I would be getting paid, with a friend, most probably his drinking partner. He would gesture, through our office window, for me to come out. I would have to hand him over my pay packet which contained notes and coins, visible through a clear window, stapled, in order to secure the notes. I was not even allowed to open my own pay packet.

He would buy his whisky, with this money, and may be a bit of food. Before the end of the following week, all the money would be gone.

Occasionally, my parents would drive to my work place, in order to physically see me, to make sure I was alright. They would hand me some cash, which I was to use in an emergency, or towards Sonal's food. They would also hand over a bag of new clothes for her as she was growing up fast, and I was unable to buy her any new clothes.

I felt so isolated, not being able to see my parents and my brothers, and my sisters-in- law, who were like sisters to me, before I had got married.

The only people I was able to see was my sister, Rakish, and her husband. He got on well with them, though he was usually sober and at his best behaviour when he saw them. We would often go and visit them in Leighton Buzzard, or they would come and visit us.

He was a likeable person when sober, no doubt about that. We had some good times together, but his heavy drinking addiction was the problem, and out of control.

Once, I had finished a day at work, picked Sonal from her childminder, I parked the car in the carpark outside our flats. He grabbed my car keys, and left in a hurry. In a couple of hours, he rushed home, telling me to ring the police and tell them that my car had been stolen. Within those two hours, he had got drunk and driven my car into some stationary cars, in the Langley High street, and then left the scene, abandoning the car at the scene of the accident.

I refused to lie for him, but he got aggressive and started threatening me. So, I rang the police station and told them that my car had been stolen, and gave them all the necessary details.

After I had done that, I shouted at him, saying that, I no longer had a car to go to work, and to take Sonal to the childminder. How were we to manage without the car?

He did not like me talking to him in the tone I had used, so he started punching me. He took off his wooden clog that he used to wear in the house, and hit me on my head with it.

I lost consciousness from the blow on my head. When I came to, he had been dabbing my blood on my cut head with a tea towel. My hair was all matted up with blood.

He kept saying 'sorry'. I held Sonal tight, tears in my eyes, for I thought that I was going to die. She was crying too, not sure what was happening.

Luckily, I survived the blow, and was left with a sore bump on the back of my head.

I had to ring my workplace to tell them that I would not be coming in the next few days. I lied to them, saying that I had had a fall and hurt my head whilst painting the kitchen.

The police rang to say that they could not find the culprit who had caused the accident, and that they had removed the car from the scene, and taken it to a scrapyard.

After that call, I heard nothing about the car or its whereabouts.

We ended up buying a tatty old Mini, to replace our car.

When I did return to work, my work mates were concerned about the fall I had. I told them a lie again, saying that I had been standing on the kitchen worktop, painting the wall, when I slipped and fell, thus cut my head, and that I had to have stitches.

One of my colleagues, who was a trained First Aider, wanted to check my wound to see how it was healing. But I would not let him near me, as I was worried that he would notice that I had no stitches on my cut.

I kind of sussed that they all knew that I had lied and that I was living with a violent partner.

They had seen him come to my work place to collect my wages, each week. They had also seen my parents come to see me at work and hand me some money, whereas they could have easily visited me at home.

They knew, but were waiting for me to say something, which I didn't, out of shame.

I managed to fall pregnant with my second daughter, Sirita, and she was born on 30th May 1981.

I had to leave my job at Heathrow Cold Store. One of my colleagues came over to see my new baby, and also brought with her my Maternity Allowance. I was going to be getting this allowance for several weeks. She would bring this money over to me during this period.

I did not disclose this money to Arun. Suddenly I felt so rich. I would hide it, where he could not find it, and I would only dip into it in an emergency.

My sister, Rakish, brought over eleven different outfits and toys for Sirita. I had enough clothes to get me going for a while.

Before the birth of Sirita, my Didi had also given birth to her second child, a baby boy. She had fallen very ill after the birth, and was diagnosed with a heart problem.

My brother-in-law sent for my mother-in-law from India, to come over to care for the baby and Didi.

Whilst she was over, she would come to visit us too. In fact, she was present at the hospital, the day I gave birth to Sirita.

After the birth of my baby, the placenta did not expel, so it had to be physically removed by the Gynaecologist. There was so much pain, worse than the labour pain, and I must have passed out during this procedure. Or perhaps I had been given an anaesthetic. This is when I believe that I had an out of body experience.

I saw myself on the delivery bed, with the Surgeon and two nurses looking over me. It was as if I was looking down at us from the ceiling. It could have been a hallucination, but when I came to, I was told that they had almost lost me. My mother-in-law, whom I would in a way of respect call her 'Chai' and Arun also said the same.

Chai would visit us whenever she could, and during these times, she noticed the behaviour in her son, when drunk. She also noticed that he mistreated me. She would console me whenever I was distressed, but was scared to confront him as he would be rude to her.

See, in Arun's books, he was never wrong, it was always the other person's fault.

I made a great bond with Chai, and she was always kind and understanding towards me.

There was an incident, when Arun had taken Chai and Sonal in the car for a drive somewhere. He was speeding and driving recklessly when he had to brake hard. Sonal went flying in the back in the footwall. Luckily, she was not hurt, but Chai ended up with a broken arm. She was taken to hospital and ended up with a cast on one of her arms.

This caused a lot of problem, as she could not help Didi and her new born, the purpose for which she had come over in the first place.

When she had recovered from her injury, it was time for her to go back to India. Since Didi was not fit enough to look after her baby, and having to make numerous trips to hospitals for her heart problem, it was decided that her baby be taken to India, and be looked after by Chai.

Trip to Jalandhar

We got an invite from Chai to attend my younger brother-in-law's wedding in India. Somehow we managed to get tickets for the journey. We did a bit of necessary shopping for the trip. We bought the girls some new dresses for the wedding. Sonal was about three years of age by now and Sirita, about five months.

I asked Arun to bring out the little jewellery I had left from the safe at the bank, where we had deposited it, to wear at the wedding. But when he took me over to the bank, the deposit box was empty, apart from a gold chain Chai had given me.

My parents had given Arun about five Krugerrands, the South African gold coins, as a gift when we had got married. They were all gone too.

He had never let me near the deposit box before, and I had believed that the jewellery and the Krugerrands were safely sitting there. I was wrong. He had blown it all.

We managed to travel to India, ending up at Chai's house. It was a three storey, old house with a courtyard on the ground floor, where the kitchen was situated.

The first floor was where all the bedrooms were, and the top floor was occupied by my late father-in-law's brother's family.

We were sharing this house with my three brothers-in-law, one of whom had a wife and a young daughter.

I was welcomed by my new family and they made an effort to keep us comfortable.

This would only be a few weeks, as I was told that there was a new house being built and the family were going to move into it, before the wedding. Apart from the uncle who lived on the top floor, who was going to end up living in that house with his young family.

The new house was in a lovely, modern colony. It had plenty of rooms, with a huge courtyard. The house was surrounded by a wall and had a main gate. There were stairs leading up to the terrace.

Soon, we all moved into the new house, and started preparing for my brother-in-law's wedding.

Chai bought me a beautiful saree, to be worn at the wedding. One of the eldest brothers-in-law gave me some golden bangles and a necklace to be worn for the occasion. Both the saree and the jewellery matched his wife's. I felt so special, the way they made me feel equal, and treated me to the new saree, for I didn't have any appropriate outfits to wear.

The wedding was to take place in Jammu in Kashmir, just over two hundred miles from Jalandhar.

Most of the relatives, ended up travelling to Jammu on a hired coach. But I was in a car with Chai, my Didi Maya's six-month old son, who had been previously sent to India to be cared for by Chai, due to her poor health, my older sister-in-law with her young daughter, and my two daughters.

The wedding was lavish, nothing I had experienced before. There was a lot of singing, dancing and food. The groom had arrived at the wedding on a horse back that was in its full regalia, a brass band playing wedding tunes in front of the groom's horse, with all the guests following behind him on foot, placing garlands, made out of rupee notes, around his neck, in a form of gift, congratulating him as they did so.

Chai had hired a couple of child minders to take care of our young children, so that we would be left free to enjoy the wedding. This helped us, mothers, a lot, especially, when it was quite late in the day, and the children were ready for a sleep.

When the wedding was over, we all drove back to Jalandhar. The relatives and friends by the same coach that had brought them over, and the new bride and groom in a separate car, which had been decorated with garlands of flowers.

The newlywed couple were to live in Delhi, where my brother-in-law had a flat, all furnished and ready for them to start their married life and also, where he had his business , once the few traditional ceremonies had been performed.

Arun was at his best behaviour, since we arrived in India. I was always around the women in the house, and he was either with his brothers or out catching up with his old friends he had left behind, when coming over to England, so there was less chance of us having any arguments.

This all changed, when he decided to go back home to England. I wanted to stay a bit longer, as I was having a great time with my new family.

He booked his flight, which was to leave from Delhi airport. He moved in with my younger brother-in-law in his Delhi flat.

On the day he was supposed to fly, he got drunk at the airport, and somehow he slipped and ended up breaking his leg. He could not fly back home, for his leg was in a cast.

The news soon got to us in Jalandhar, and a demand that I come to Delhi to care for him.

I was driven there the next day, in the car the family had just bought. I was driven to Delhi by their driver, as the rest of the family could not drive yet, accompanied by my youngest brother-in-law.

As soon as we got to the flat, Arun was in a foul mood. He was angry that he had broken his leg, he was angry that I had not been there for him, when it happened. And that his brother with his new wife did not pamper him.

I was sat opposite him on a sofa, next to the youngest brother-in-law, when suddenly he got hold of the hockey stick he had been using to get about due to his broken leg, and banged it on the wooden coffee table. He shouted at us to sit apart. This came as a great shock to us, and my young brother-in-law got up and left the room. Soon I was verbally abused by Arun, calling me all sorts of names.

This behaviour of his carried on for weeks, and his family noticed it too. They were all getting fed up of it, and sympathised with me for having to put up with it.

One day, when his demands were not fulfilled, he threatened to jump off the balcony of the third floor of the flats where we lived. My brother-in-law ignored his threat, so Arun simply came and sat down on the sofa, and muttered that nobody cared if he were dead. Once again he was seeking attention.

He realised that he could not push everyone about, like he did with me. I felt safe with all the family around me and my daughters. I did not wish to go back home. Back to the abuse, where I had no one to protect me.

He soon got uneasy with his cast, and decided to remove it himself. And now that he was free of it, he rebooked his flight to England and left.

I stayed at the Delhi flat for a while, as there was no one available to take me back to Jalandhar, and Chai did not want me to travel on my own with my two kids.

For some reason, the newlyweds had to go away for a while, perhaps on their honeymoon, I don't really recall the real reason, and I was left to my own device with the girls, to stay at their flat.

I would go to the local shop which was situated right next to the flat, to get the grocery. There was a lady, that ran a tandoor next to the grocery shop, where I would take some flour dough, and she would cook me some tandoori rotis.

There was a vegetable seller, who would sell his vegetables on a cart, pulled by his bike.

When I heard his loud voice, shouting, 'carrots, fresh tomatoes, cauliflower, potatoes, etc.' I would run to the back window and shout back, for him to stop for me. Then I would shout back the vegetables I wanted to buy. I would dangle down my basket that was tied to a long rope with the money and he would place the veg's in the basket, with any loose change. I would then pull back the basket on the rope. This was ideal, when there was no other adult in the house, for me not having to drag my two girls, all the way down the stairs.

Soon my Chai came to Delhi to keep me company.

There was a traditional occasion associated with the goddess Devi Mata, when young unmarried girls are invited over for a feast, and are treated like a Devi, meaning a goddess in

Sanskrit. Chai wanted me to host this occasion. I would have to cook the meal. Then when the Devis arrived, wash their feet before serving them the meal, and then giving them gifts of money and a red scarf.

I prepared all the food, apart from the pudding, which was supposed to be 'Krah' which is a semolina pudding.

I told Chai that I had never made this before. She was kind enough to make it herself.

When all the young Devis arrived, accompanied by their mothers, one of them being Chai's sister,

Chai told them that I had cooked the meal, and when praised by them for the lovely pudding, she told them that I had cooked that as well.

I felt overwhelmed by her kindness.

I returned to Jalandhar with Chai and spent some great days with her and the rest of the family. I would go to places with Arun's cousins for meals or shopping. I would hop on the back of my younger brother-in-law's scooter and go for a ride with him, taking in all the scenery around Jalandhar city.

I was having a great time, no worries of being taunted by my husband.

But then he started phoning up asking me to return home, back to England. He said that he couldn't cope on his own, and wanted me back as soon as possible.

I had to book my flight home, and left India with my young daughters.

A New Home

We decided to apply to the Council for a bigger place to live, as Sirita was turning one, and Sonal was almost three years of age. We were all sharing one bedroom in our flat.

We soon got an offer of a property in Wexham in Slough. It was a semi-detached house, with a long drive and a garden in the front. A huge garden at the back of the house, surrounded by a privet hedge, running from one end of the house to the other. The back garden was divided into two parts. The first half was a lawn, and then, through a wooden gate, led to an orchard. We had apple trees and pear trees, bearing fruit, and there were beds of vegetables and strawberries.

The front garden too had an apple tree, so large that its branches were reaching the front bedroom window.

I was not able to work, with two young girls to look after, but I managed to find a part time job that suited me at the time selling Avon cosmetics.

I would drop the brochures door to door, then collect them and place the orders. This gave me a little income. But still not enough to make ends meet.

Life was getting tough, with a husband not working, and supporting his family. Instead blowing any money coming in the form of child benefit and the help from the Government, towards his drinking. Whenever I tried to intervene, there would be another row, followed with a fight.

He was not paying the bills regularly. We were running into so much debt. We would get reminder letters, which he would blatantly ignore. This ended up us getting an eviction notice from the council to vacate our house by a certain date or settle the monies owed to them. Failing to pay them the bailiffs came to the door on the set date and asked us to vacate the property immediately. They started changing the locks, so that we would not try entering the property.

We were thrown out of our house with just a few belongings, and milk and food for the girls that we could carry.

We were given a condition, that if we were able to settle the debt before the end of that day, we would be able to move back in.

We drove around, from one friend to another, begging to help us, but no one was prepared to help.

Then Arun rang his brother up and begged him to help us out.

He was kind enough to handover the money to us within a couple of hours, despite all the disputes we had in the past.

We rushed to the council to pay back the debt and were allowed to move back home.

On one occasion, we had had a row, so I went and lay down with my two girls.

He didn't like me ignoring him, so he came into the girls' bedroom, dragged me out of bed, and started pushing me towards the stairs, whilst shouting abuse at me. As I got to the bottom of the stairs, he opened the front door and pushed me out, closing the door behind him.

It was pouring down with rain. I had not even had a chance to grab any coat, sweater or shoes, so I started banging on the door, for him to let me in.

There was no chance of that. He did not even have a heart. He always had things going his way, no one else mattered.

I had no choice, but to look for the nearest phone box and ring my parents.

I ran to the street behind our house, towards Wexham Hospital, which was about fifteen minutes' walk from our house. The rain was getting very heavy by now. My clothes and my hair were drenched.

My feet were cut from the concrete paths. Some cars passed by and a few people walked past me. They stared at me, perhaps thinking, that I was an escapee from the mental wards of the Wexham hospital.

I reached the public telephone box that was situated outside the main road of the hospital. I rang my parents, by reverse calling. My dad answered the phone, but could not understand what I was saying. One reason being that he had been woken from his sleep, secondly I was weeping, as I tried to tell him, what had just happened and lastly, the noise from traffic and the heavy rain made it difficult for him to hear me properly.

At last, he heard me saying that I was outside the Wexham Hospital, and I wanted him to pick me up. He said that he would be there as soon as he could.

I waited for him for what seemed like hours, inside the telephone box, trying to avoid getting drenched and also avoid the stares from the passersby.

I saw his car drive by, accompanied by my mum. But they didn't see me, due to the heavy rain. They had driven into the hospital, and asked around, if they had seen me.

Failing to find me in there, they drove out of the hospital, and as I noticed their car again, I stepped outside of the telephone box and started waving at them. Luckily, they noticed me this time.

My parents were so shocked to find me in the condition I was in. My mum started crying her eyes out as I told them of my ordeal.

My mum was so annoyed about the situation, that in anger, she asked my dad to drive to my Didi and brother-in-law's house, so that they could see how I was being treated by Arun.

We got to the house, and my mum held me by my arm, and the three of us walked to the door.

My brother-in-law answered the door, followed by Didi.

My mum shouted, "Look at the sight of our daughter, look how your brother has been treating her! He has chucked her out, without any shoes in the heavy rain."

At that moment, in my head, I was thinking, how ashamed I was, to be seen in this condition.

I was also, not hoping, but thinking, that my Didi will take me in her arms, and wrap a shawl over my wet, shivering body, and lend me her warm slippers.

But as soon as she saw me, she told my parents, that she wanted nothing to do with me, and that I had made my bed, and should lie on it.

Upon hearing this, I ran back to my dad's car, and sobbed my eyes out, while my parents still tried talking sense in to them, but it was all in vain.

We drove to my parents' flat, where my mum gave me some clothes to change into. They were too big on me, and I looked like a clown in them.

Arun had left numerous messages on their phone, saying that he wanted me to return home, as the girls were asking for me. My dad rang him back and had some stern words with him. To which Arun promised that he would not hurt me again, and that he was going to stop drinking.

I did not wish to return back to him, but I was worried about my girls, being alone with a monster of a dad.

So, the next day, I was driven back home.

Once again all the promises were broken, the circle continued. We had some good days, but generally bad days. I often wondered if this was going to be my life for ever. I felt trapped. There was no escape. My parents were helpless too. I hardly talked to my brothers about my problems out of shame and because he had made me cut ties with them.

My parents would secretly meet me and give me some money, in case I had an emergency.

I would roll the notes like a thin cigarette and hide them in the holes in the pointings on the outside walls of our house, just so that if I was thrown out of the house again, I would have access to that money at least.

I was invited to my niece's birthday party, by my sister, Rakish. My brother-in-law came to pick me and my girls up from Leighton Buzzard. For some reason, Arun did not join us.

We had a great party, and my girls were so happy to play with their cousins.

While we were there, Arun kept on ringing, asking us to return home. My sister suggested that we would be brought home once the party was over.

He was not happy that I was having a good time with my family, without him, so he rang again and threatened that he was going to drive over, and ruin the party.

So, my brother-in-law drove us back home, along with his two daughters, so that they would have a chance to spend more time with my girls.

As we reached our home, we all went in. Arun was upstairs in our bedroom. All the girls went into my girls' room to play, and my brother-in-law and I went up to our bedroom to see Arun. He was sat on the bed, bottle of whisky and a tumbler on the bedside table, his eyes red from drink. My brother-in-law took the chair in the room, and I sat on the floor, leaning my back against the wall. I could smell the drink on his breath, yet he was polite enough. The three of us talked for a while.

When it was time for them all to go, my brother-in-law went to use the loo.

While he was out of the room, Arun started punching me and kicking me, accusing me of all sorts Of things. My brother-in-law confronted him, but he pushed him and came after me as I ran downstairs to the kitchen. All the girls were crying and were scared, with all the commotion going on. Specially Sirita, who was screaming by now. My brother-in-law brought her over to me in the kitchen, so I could calm her down, and then went up to see to the three panicked girls.

This gave Arun a chance to come after me in the kitchen. He took a knife from the kitchen drawer and started waving it at me and threatening me with it. I was screaming by now, in fear of what he might do. He came closer, waving the knife about, and ended up giving Sirita a small cut on her leg.

I made a great haste towards the front door, in order to escape him, Sirita in my arms. By this time my brother-in-law had come down too, and asked me to run out of the house and hide, while he confronted him again. The three girls too ran out of the house, and my brother-in-law, somehow escaped Arun and ran out of the house. He gathered the three girls in his car, and was met by the police, who had suddenly arrived at the scene. I believe the next door neighbours had phoned them, after hearing all the screaming and shouting going on.

I came out of my hiding place, when I saw the police arriving, and saw Arun being taken away by the police. I too was taken to the police station to give a statement, and have photos taken of the bruises to my body. They told me that Arun had been arrested.

My brother-in-law returned to his house, with his daughters, when all had settled down.

I was told by the police, that I would have to let him in the house to take all his belongings, before I would be allowed to move in, and that he was given an injunction, not to return to the property after that.

When I was allowed back in our property, I was always nervous, and looking over my shoulder, in case Arun returned. The girls were always nervous too.

In fact Sonal had had a few slaps and beatings from him, if she did something wrong, due to which she had ended up having a lazy eye, which had never been apparent at birth.

She also lost the ability of speech that a four and half-years child would have, and started babbling along, not making sense of her speech.

She ended up having sessions with a speech therapist, and had an operation to have her lazy eye corrected.

He had taken all his belongings, so there shouldn't be any chance of him returning. He also took the car we used to share.

Strangely enough, while he had been given access to the house for removing his belongings, my Avon order had arrived. He had the audacity to pack all the orders in individual bags for the customers, and delivered the goods to them, pocketing the money. That proved to me, how low this man could fall.

He had seen me pack the orders so many times, he knew exactly what to do.

I struggled to pay back the money into my Avon account that he had pocketed.

There is a funny incident that took place, when the speech therapist had requested for me to let her come and assess Sonal in our house, in her familiar surroundings. She wanted to see how she behaved in her own environment compared to the small office she was normally seen in.

Before the meeting date, I panicked about the girls' bedroom. I thought that the therapist would be surprised to see that Sonal slept in a double bed I had inherited from family, next to Sirita's cot. I had normally seen children her age in a single bed, or bunk beds. So, I stripped the bed, cut the wooden frame into half, and then laboriously untangled the springs of the bed. Then dressed it up to make it look like a single bed.

It looked good, but every time the girls stepped on the side that had been cut, the bed would tilt.

At least her therapist was happy to see her play happily, with the few toys and books she had in her bedroom. I was so glad that she had not sat on the 'half bed', but the chair I had provided her with.

My siblings still have a belly laugh to this date when we talk about the funny incident.

The girls were making friends with the neighbourhood children, most of who went to the same school as Sonal, and would play with them on the green opposite our house, where I could keep an eye on them, from my window.

There were particular neighbourhood kids, a brother and sister, who would always hang around the front of our house, wanting to play with the girls. The boy must have been about five and the girl about eight years of age. They were beautiful kids, with blue eyes and blond hair, but appeared to be poorly dressed, with shabby clothes, and their hair unkempt. They would often remove their shoes whilst playing, and I would notice that the soles of their feet would be black with dirt, and there would also be dirt between their toes.

Soon I met up with their mother, when she came over, looking for her kids. She said that her name was Mary.

She too seemed to be a bit untidy.

She started visiting me regularly. While the children played on the green, we would sit on my doorstep with a cup of tea and biscuits. She told me that she loved reading books, and from her chats, she seemed very knowledgeable about books.

Then one day she started reciting a poem she had thought up herself. I was very impressed and asked her to jot it on a piece of paper for me.

I fetched some paper and pen, and she carefully picked the words she needed to jot down, looking up in the sky, as if that's where her answers lay and that's where she would find the appropriate words, mumbled a few words and then wrote the poem on the paper.

I was very impressed indeed, as she was thinking of the rhyming words in front of my eyes and came up with a great poem. She let me keep it.

She wrote one more after that and let me keep that too. I feel that I should present them, not to take the credit myself, but to not let her talent go unnoticed.

I have kept these pages of her talent all these years, and wanted to share them.

These are the poems Mary wrote.

First Poem

>*I am wondering through a wonderland,*
>*Is it true love I have found?*
>*Or maybe it's a dream, this wonderland*
>*Oh! This familiar road, I am bound.*
>
>*It should be time for joy and madness*
>*But oft it is time of sadness*
>*"Parting is such sweet sorrow," someone said*
>*I know what they meant, when I lay in my bed.*
>
>*There are other famous sayings, I know them so well,*
>*About Parting, good-byes, and the fond farewells.*
>*"Out of sight, out of mind," is not true for me*
>*"Absence makes the heart grow fonder," yes I agree.*

But love of my life, we soldier on still,
We care for each other, which gives us a thrill.
Each needing the other, for friendship and love
Well it must be Heaven sent from above.

You're like a Greek God, from the history book pages
Does it spoil it, that we are different ages?
You are young and virile, with features so strong
And when I'm in your arms, I feel I belong.

We say loving words at the height of passion
And we play our special songs, which are all the fashion
But we mean what we say, at least at the time
We don't have to hold back or draw the line.

Who dares to question our love and our joy?
After all I'm a girl and you are a boy.
Our feelings will last as long as they're meant to
When at last it must end, we'll know what to do.

What I miss most when we are apart
Is the fact that I can't hold you close to my heart?
Were you there in the morning, and again at night?
Did you love me, Kiss me and hold me tight?

Let's live for today, tomorrow we die,
Our lives are short, like the butterfly.
We are sent here to love, and love we must.
Be loving and faithful, but above all trust.

Second Poem

My man, he is the special kind,
Yet I don't love him for his mind.
He has got special qualities, that something more,
He is very special, of that I'm sure.

He's loving and thoughtful, funny as well,
And I know he would catch me if ever I fell.
He's kindness itself and considerate too,
Anything you ask, he will do.

I call him my man, he is not really at all
He's a free spirit who'd come if I should call.
I wish he were mine, to have and to hold,
But he is young and single, not to be told.

He's warm and he's tender, he's loving and kind,
With eyes that seem to look inside of my mind.
He has the heart of a lion, the hug of a bear,
But deep down inside he's a lamb, oh so rare.

Oh my man, I love him so,
If only there was a way of letting him know.
A hundred years have passed or so it would seem,
Why doesn't he return? We'd make a good team.

So here I must sit and wait patiently,
For my man to come home to me.
He has the power, the key to my heart,
Please god look after him, while we are apart.

Written by Mary Rushton

Mary had an amazing talent. Reading her poems, I felt like she had been in love, and been hurt.

Before I had a chance to know more about her and her past, for like me, she was single and a mother to two kids, she told me that she was going to move to Herne Bay in Kent.

I never saw her again, and she never left me with her forwarding address.

A new Freedom

Despite going through all the trauma and abuse, I was kind of relieved that it was all in the open.

No one had actually witnessed the abuse I had suffered, till now. I had been previously accused of being a drama queen. But my brother-in-law having witnessed what had happened, saved me from an abusive relationship.

When the rest of the family came to hear of the horrid episode, I was able to see my brothers, and their families again. I was also able to visit my parents. One of my brothers gave me encouragement to file for divorce. He found me a great lawyer, who speeded up with all the formalities.

When Sonal turned five she started her primary education, and I put Sirita in a play group. Both the school and the nursery were very close to our house.

During my walks to the school, I made friends with a few mums.

At Sirita's play group, there used to be a young dad, who would drop his son to the play group. I soon found that he was a single parent, and lived with his mum, since his wife had left him. We got talking once, as we walked back home, and he told me that he was a member of the Salvation Army.

And when he learned that I was a single parent too with two young girls he arranged for me to receive food parcels delivered to my house by the Salvation Army. There would be vegetables, tinned food, sweets, fruit, crisps and various other goodies. This helped me a lot.

I had been left with debts, by Arun, for gas, electricity and various other bills, along with the never ending loan from the loan shark which I had to pay back in instalments, arranged for me by the providers.

I was struggling financially, but there was peace at last.

I would keep myself busy with the household chores.

I also managed to buy a second -hand push bike from the car boot sale, and would ride to town and back with shopping resting on the handle bars.

I would cut the grass, and prune the privet hedge from one end of the house to the other, and by the time I reached the end, the previously cut hedge would be growing already. It was a never-ending task.

I was having some plumbing fixed by the council one day, and the engineer had left the main door open, for access to his tools. Suddenly, Arun walked into the house, and started chatting to him, like he still lived there. I was so scared and demanded that he left, or I would call the authorities.

Luckily, he left without causing a scene. This made me very nervous, as he was so unpredictable and could come over anytime to haunt me and my girls.

He had also previously turned up at Sonal's School, demanding to be allowed to see her. The school had rung me and alerted me. The school had been informed not to allow anyone, but me, to pick her up. They were aware of my circumstances, so he was refused access to see her.

These two incidents, made me very uneasy, and I decided that the best way to keep safe would be to move house. One of the mums from the playschool, who had befriended me, had seen an advert in the window of the local newsagent, with someone wanting to swap their property and asked me to try ringing them. I rang the number, and arranged to go and view the property which was in Maidenhead.

I asked my parents to take me there. I loved the house, which had an open plan living room, three bedrooms. There was a decent front garden and a very beautifully manicured, and established back garden, just big enough for me to maintain. I loved the house, and arranged for the couple to view my property.

They came over the next day and then rang me that evening to say that they were happy to swap, if I was. They came over for a second viewing. When they arrived, they immediately started measuring up for curtains and walls, and floors, as if already planning their soft furnishings.

We both agreed to set a date for the swap, at the end of the following month.

I was helped by the authorities to move. There was not a lot of furniture, just one van full.

My friend was very excited for me, as it was due to her recommendation that I went ahead with the idea of the swap.

It was a pity that I never saw her again when I moved to Maidenhead. It was a sad fact that I didn't try to keep in touch with her, on the phone at least.

She had also advised me that I should change my name by deed poll, so that my ex-husband would never be able to trace me.

After consulting with my brother and the lawyer, I went ahead with the idea.

I would sit there with a pad and a pen jotting down the names I could choose from. Then I opted for the name "Kiran". It was nice and short, compared to "Ravinder".

I also decided to change my surname, as I didn't want to carry Arun's surname. So now my new name was "Kiran Raj".

I always loved the name Kiran. It was nice and short. I picked the second name as 'Raj' as I had always been a fan of the Bollywood legend, Raj Kapoor. He mostly played parts resembling Charlie Chaplin though some of his movies were based on real lives people tend to experience. I always made sure that I didn't miss any of his movies.

Once I had adopted my new name, I sat and practised my signature, over and over.

We settled in our new home. Sonal, was admitted in the local primary school, which was a walking distance, and Sirita started playgroup.

I had an urge one day to contact my old friend, Mr Cockburn. I tried dialling his phone number, wondering if he would still have the same number. Fortunately he did answer my call.

He was surprised, and yet delighted to hear from me, as we had not been in touch since I left my job at B.O.C.

I told him about my divorce and that I had two lovely daughters.

He was sad to hear of my news, but also said that it was inevitable, as I had been married to a stranger. The fact that he could not digest.

He said that he would like to meet me, so we could talk in depth.

We planned to meet up at the Black Park in Wexham, in Slough.

We walked around the beautiful park, while I told him of my ordeal.

He felt very sad for me, and hoped that I would try and sort my life out, and wished me luck.

As we walked along, he started pointing out to various trees and telling me their names. Then he would ask me to point out at the trees, as he named them to test me out.

He couldn't help himself. As usual he was still trying to educate me.

I never saw him after that, apart from a few phone calls, from which I learned that the offices where we worked in Brentford had moved. The other fact could have been that he had retired by now, and moved to Scotland, where I recall him telling me about a property he had, and used to spend most summer holidays at.

I would walk to Maidenhead town, in order to familiarise myself with the area. All I needed was to find a part time job that would fit in, with the girls' school times. Money was scarce, with the outstanding debts.

My parents would often visit me, and bring us food parcels.

My dad would give me his collection of twenty pence pieces, which he had saved in his twenty pence coin saving gadget, for me to feed the electric meter.

There was a young dad called Paz who used to drop his son at the same play group as Sirita's. We got chatting and I mentioned about finding a part time job. He was working for a local mini cab company as a driver, where they were in need of a base operator. He made arrangements for me to see his boss the next day. I was interviewed by him, and he demonstrated the operation of the workings of a base operating. He was happy to give me the job, and I started the next day which was in June 1986.

It was practical, and flexible for me, as the house he operated his business from was on the way to Sonal's school. She would walk home from school to his house, with some of her friends, then we would walk home from there. I was even allowed to take Sirita with me to work, after her playschool time was over.

He was very kind to us. He would feed my girls after school time, if I was still busy working, and there were times when my kids would be picked up from school, by one of his drivers, if it was raining.

My now boss, Mr Ahmed, had two boys and a daughter. His wife had gone to Pakistan to visit her family, hence he needed me there to cover the job that she used to do

I would often see Paz, at the base, between his jobs. I was thankful to him for finding me a job.

I carried on working for Mr Ahmed even after his wife returned from Pakistan as she was pregnant and needed to take things easy.

Soon I found that he had a drink problem, and would often stay in pubs, in the evenings, with friends instead of running his business.

I had to leave the job as he could not afford to keep me, and I found out that his business had failed and he lost his house too.

Paz approached me and announced that he was going to form his own mini cab company, and that he would like me to go and work for him. I was delighted to hear that, as I already had experience in base operating.

When his company was finally formed, he asked me to work for him, not as an operator but as a driver. I was shocked to hear that and told him that this was not what I had been expecting. But he insisted, and promised that I would be trained and helped at every stage.

His sister was going to be working as a base operator, and he was in need of drivers. He would be running his company from his dad's house, which he and his brothers were sharing.

I gave it a long thought and decided to give it a go.

I was provided with a company car, equipped with a CB radio.

I soon picked up the job, with a lot of help and used a local map book to find my way around, till I got familiar with the area, and became confident. My code name was Lima four, as I was the fourth driver to join the company. Paz was obviously Lima one.

I would only work during school hours. So, this job was ideal for me.

I had had a few minor accidents with the cabs though, as it had been a long time since I had driven a car.

Once I ended up in a hedge, while going around a sharp corner, getting a cut on my chin, and it was bleeding. I had to get in touch with the base to tell them that I had been in an accident.

They sent a car over, with a driver to pick me up, and Paz, followed him in order to sort out the car I had just smashed.

I was taken back to the base, as I didn't need any emergency treatment.

Paz's dad fussed over me, asked his daughter to make me a cup of tea, and also dressed my wound.

I had to play up a bit and pretend that I was in a shock, as I was so ashamed that I had smashed their car therefore ended up getting sympathy, instead of a telling off.

All the other drivers were concerned too and sympathised with me, when they were at the base between jobs.

When it was time to pick up my daughters from school, they sent a driver to fetch them from school and bring them to the base, while I rested and was fit enough to return home.

Paz's mum fed my girls, along with her grandchildren.

I was very thankful to the whole family, for showing us such kindness.

Soon Paz's sister got married and left the family house to live with her in-laws, and her brother-in-law along with Paz's dad started operating the base. Her new husband too started driving for the company, and the business started flourishing, and they were recruiting more drivers.

After a few months' training, I was being sent to the airports and London, and other parts of the country. I had to extend my hours too.

I had a neighbour called Bridie, who was happy to have my girls after school, till I finished work, for a small fee. She was very helpful, as she would feed the girls if I rang her to tell her that I would be late. She had a teenage son and a daughter, so they kept my girls entertained.

I was going places in my job, and meeting all kinds of people. I was often favoured by older ladies, who felt safe me picking them up. In fact, there was a lovely lady who unfortunately was in a wheel chair. She had a family wedding to attend in Chichester in West Sussex. So, she requested that I took her there and back.

Then there was another lady who too requested that I took her to Gloucestershire to see her nephew, who was at a Monastery. I got a chance to see the Prink Nash Abbey, and purchase some pottery that was made by the monks.

The farthest journey I ever made during my mini-cabbing, was from Cookham, Berkshire to Middlesbrough.

Paz would favour me some times and secretly send me on jobs that he had directly taken calls to.

He would send me to Gatwick or Heathrow Airport, so that I could earn more money.

Well! I suppose he was the boss, so I suppose he could do this.

I was caught once though, when I had travelled to the Gatwick airport to pick up a fare that Paz had asked me to. This was supposed to be one of our secret jobs. I waited for the passenger to come through the gate, holding a card with his name on it, and clutching on to my first ever mobile phone, a Retro brick phone. I waited and waited, but he never appeared. I later found that he had already been picked up by another driver, as he had called the base, to make sure that a driver was being sent to pick him up. I ended up coming home without a fare. That taught Paz and me a lesson, not to take risks.

Soon Paz suggested that I bought my own cab, as this would help me earn more money. All I would have to do was, to pay towards the CB radio, and all the money I earned would be mine.

He helped me with the purchase of a car for which I had to pay in instalments.

He introduced me to his accountant, who only charged me a minimal fee for his services.

So now I was all set to be self-employed.

My first car was a Nissan Bluebird. It was all kitted out with a CB radio, ready to go.

I preferred having my own car as I used to be given whatever car was available before, and I had to leave it at the base during the weekends, when I wasn't working.

It also gave me the freedom of going to see my family and my parents.

Paz was always trying his best to build up his business by introducing his services to some local companies and hotels. He would sometimes treat the clients to a meal, in order to get their contracts.

He once asked me if I would like to accompany him to one of these meals, as the client was going to bring his wife along. Paz's wife was a simple Pakistani lady. She could not read or write English. She also dressed in her traditional dress. There was no way that she would be prepared to be taken out for a meal, to meet some clients.

I agreed to accompany him.

We met the couple at a local restaurant, and Paz treated us all to a meal and drinks. The client, a Mr Graham Scott, was happy for us to provide his company with our taxi service.

I often picked Graham up, and dropped him at various places, after that. He once invited Paz and myself to join him at a Casino in Reading.

I was so nervous to go, as I didn't have any posh clothes to wear. So, I hired a beautiful black sequins dress for the day, which I later found to be a waste of money, as most of the women at the casino were in their smart casuals.

I had imagined it to be like what one sees in the movies, with the ladies in their beautifully cut dresses and furs.

At least I had had the chance of going to a Casino.

I remember picking Graham up once, and he asked me about my family. I told him that I was a single parent with two teenage girls. Then he asked me where I would be taking my girls for their summer holiday, as the summer holiday term was approaching. To which I replied that I could not afford to take them anywhere.

He said that he felt sorry for us, not being able to go on holiday, and would love to pay for a holiday for us.

I blatantly refused, and told him that I would rather save up and only take the girls away when I could afford it.

He could not have imagined, what I had gone through in my married life. My girls and I had gone without food, and had gone through physical and mental abuse by my ex-husband. A holiday was the last thing on my mind.

All the debts and bills had to be settled before I could think of having a holiday.

He said that he was proud of me, for my principles. And that if ever I needed any help, he would be happy to help.

I took him up on his offer, when Sonal had to find some work experience at school. I rang him and asked him, if he could offer her some work experience. He gladly agreed, and let her work in his company for a week. He also kindly paid her for the work she had done.

I was enjoying meeting people, and having a bit of a social life, in my job. I was also building up my confidence now that I knew that my ex-husband could never trace me, with my new place to live and a new identity.

I would go to the base, between jobs and chat and exchange notes with my fellow drivers. Sometimes I would go home, and if it happened to be my turn for a job, the base operator would give me two bells on my home phone, and I would run to the car and take the job. This helped me, as I didn't have to hang around in a layby, in my car. I could also get on with my household chores, when at home.

I would sometimes read a book, between jobs, sitting in some layby.

I was getting very popular amongst the various Mini cab companies, as at that time, in the Eighties, I must have been the only Asian mini cab driver, around Maidenhead. People would recognise me from miles, if I went shopping in town. I would forever be saying "Hello" or stopping for a chat with my customers, whom I bumped into.

I would meet up with my family, whenever there was a family occasion. My Didi and my brother-in-law would be there too, but I would be ignored by them. They wanted nothing to do with me. In fact, from what I learned at a later date from family is that my Didi would always refer to me as her biggest enemy.

If there was a party going on, she would refuse to dance, if I was on the dancing floor.

I felt really bad about this, but she was set in her ways, and was not ready to forgive me in any way.

I still loved her. After all she had not just been my sister, but my best friend in our childhood.

I also felt that, since she was not a very well person, with her heart problems, if we were on talking terms, I could have given her some form of support and help.

I was so sad, when I heard that she had had a heart transplant, later followed by a piggy back heart transplant which were carried out by the famous Heart Specialist, Dr Magdi Yacoub.

The pain and suffering she must have endured during this time. I had heard that she would drive, herself, to Harefield hospital for her appointments.

She brought up her two children so well. They ended up going to Universities.

My Dad

My dad was a victim of hypertension. He would often suffer with agonising headaches. He got treatment from the doctors to overcome it, and yet, once ended up having a heart attack. He was laid up in hospital, and was released when his blood pressure was under control.

My parents had moved from their flat, into a one- bedroom house, in Heston, Middlesex.

They had a garden in the back of the house, so my mum was able to do a bit of gardening, which was her passion, when in Uganda.

By this time my brother Ashok and Bina had moved to Peterborough, and started their family.

Gulab and Madhu along with their young daughter had moved to Swindon in Wiltshire, Rakish and her family, to Colchester whereas my eldest brother Harmesh and his family moved from Stoke-on-Trent to Northumbria.

We rarely saw our family, due to the long distances and the fact that everyone was busy in their career, and bringing up their families. We would see each other on occasions like birthdays, Christmases and Easter times.

My mum had taken her retirement soon after they had moved into their new place, and my dad was looking forward to his retirement too. His plans were to live in India, in the house he had built, most of the year.

Since moving to England, he had been feeling a bit home sick, missing his mum and brothers, in India.

He also missed the life he had in Uganda, where he had had so many friends that he would either invite over for a meal, or be invited to their parties. My mum was forever cooking and entertaining their friends. There were times, when there would be at least four to five families gathered at Entebbe, each family bringing some food, and have a great picnic.

But in England, he had not made many such friends. Everyone was busy working; his only entertainment was with the immediate family members.

After all, it must have been hard for him to come from a respectable job as a teacher where he always dressed smartly, all suited and booted, and always with a tie on, to end up working as a porter, at the airport.

The only advantage working for an airline was that he would get concession on travel. He, along with my mum travelled to India, Canada, Singapore, Germany and various other countries.

My dad's High Blood Pressure, and severe headaches caused him to take time off work, as he felt so poorly. One of his friends recommended to him an ayurvedic treatment. My dad managed to get hold of the medicines recommended, and started taking them.

My brothers and their wives had gone to visit him during Easter of 1988, on the Saturday, when they learned that he was unwell. I was planning to go and see my parents on Easter Sunday. Unfortunately, I didn't get a chance, as my dad died on Sunday. None of us were aware that he had stopped taking his prescription medication.

If only, he had not given up his prescription medication, he might have lived.

From what I learned from my mum he had hired a couple of videos to watch that night. Half way through the first film, he complained that his headache was back, and that he would go to bed and rest.

My mum carried on watching the film, and when it was over she went to see if my dad needed anything. He suggested that he just wanted to rest.

So my mum decided to watch the second film on her own, before going to bed herself.

Early Sunday morning she found that my dad was not responding, when she tried to talk to him. She panicked and the ambulance was called. My dad ended up at West Middlesex hospital in an ICU.

All our family went to the Hospital, to see him. There were so many of us around his bed, waiting for him to respond. But unfortunately, he had had a stroke and was pronounced dead on Easter Sunday. He was only 64 at the time.

We were all devastated, especially our mum, who had lost her lifetime partner. She had been very dependent on him, in every aspect of her life, as her English was not very good and he helped her in every way he could have.

After the funeral, my brothers decided that my Mother would not be able to live by herself.

So, she moved in with my brother, Ashok, and his wife Bina, in Peterborough. It was very challenging for them as they were in full time jobs, and had school age young kids, and couldn't be there for her in the daytime.

I could only speak to my mum on the phone, every now and then, as it was too far to travel, to go and see her. The only time I would see her, would be if my brother and sister-in-law would come and visit family members in London. Then they would bring her over to see me.

Mum's 60th Birthday

It was my Mum's 60th birthday, so my family decided to give her a surprise party at a venue in Slough. She was made to believe that my brothers were taking her there for tea and snacks. But soon we all started arriving, and she was overwhelmed to see all her family there.

When the party was over my brother-in-law invited everyone to his house. As I wasn't on talking terms with them, I walked towards my car, followed by Sonal and Sirita, after we had said our goodbyes. My brother-in-law came after me and invited us to join them as well. I wasn't sure what my Didi would say to that, but she said nothing.

We all gathered around in their house. I felt very awkward being there, but having the rest of the family there, put me at ease a bit.

Not long after that, I invited them over to my house, not sure if they would come. Surprisingly they accepted my invitation. They arrived with a gift of a beautiful dinner set. We talked, not about the horrid past, but the present. The ice had been broken. I would not be ignored at the family gatherings, and classed as my Didi's enemy anymore.

Soon I got the news from my family that Didi had been taken to Harefield Hospital, as her piggyback heart was giving up on her. I drove to the hospital, to visit her. I was horrified to see her condition. She could not speak, so she was writing down what she needed to say on a slate, aided by the nurses.

I felt so faint seeing her that I had to leave, tears rolling down my cheeks.

I believe that it was Easter Monday, when I got the news that she had passed away.

I was so devastated. We had only just started talking to each other. All those years wasted.

Her funeral was arranged, but I was a bit dubious about attending because I had heard from my family that my ex-husband was back on the scene, and would be at the funeral. I was not prepared to face him, even after all these years.

I asked one of my friends to accompany me, planning to get there a bit late, so that we could stay right at the back and he would not see me. That did not work out, because as we got there, everyone was just about leaving in their cars. I didn't want to step out of my car, in case I was noticed by my ex-husband.

When everyone had left, my friend and I walked over to where all the flowers had been laid by family and friends. I picked a few roses out of the flowers for keepsake. When I got home, I pressed them between the leaves of a thick book to remember my Didi by.

My brother, Gulab, and sister-in-law, Madhu decided to give Ashok and Bina a break from having my mum, and kindly moved her into their house in Swindon. Once again, they were in their full-time jobs, and could only be with her in the evenings.

She would do some gardening to keep herself occupied, and also joined the local library so she could get some Hindi books to read. She was encouraged by Madhu to learn to fetch her pension from the post office, which she could take a bus to.

Soon she was travelling on the bus, to the town centre and back on her own.

Once in a while she would stay with my sister, Rakish, and sometimes come to mine.

I loved having her over, but my girls used to complain that she cooked Indian meals all the time, and that they would like to eat their usual sausages, fish fingers and burgers sometimes. My mum would be offended if I cooked them such things.

What I would get annoyed with was, the amount of television she watched. I had subscribed to an Indian channel, and she would continuously be watching this channel, and made the girls miss out on their favourite programmes.

There were times when I would want to come home, between my jobs. But as soon as I reached my back gate, I would hear blaring music coming out of our sitting room, where she would have the volume so high, whilst watching her movies. I used to turn back and drive away.

I would read a book, sitting in a lay-by somewhere. In fact I had started reading a book by Philippa Gregory, called "The Wideacre" just before my dad had passed away. I have always related that book to that time. I carried on with the trilogy, which I enjoyed so much, I have bought and read every other book that she has written since, and always look forward to her new publications.

One good thing my mum had encouraged me to do, during her stay at my house was to pay off all the debts that I had since I divorced Arun. I used to pay the minimum payment possible, and they never seemed to end. She suggested that I give her all the money I earned each day, apart from the CB rental and petrol, and she would do all the food shopping for me. She would keep the money in a safe place, which happened to be under her mattress, till it was time to pay off my debts. I would pay bigger chunks of money towards these payments, and soon all my debts were cleared. When she came to stay over, I would normally take her to see my aunty, her sister in Cranford, and her brother and his wife in Wembley.

I had a fall out with Paz's father once. I was sitting at the base, waiting for a job. He was the only one in the office. He said that he wanted to give me some advice. His advice was that I should not wear skirts when I came to work, but should be wearing salwar kameez, which is an outfit worn by Asian women. I was very shocked to hear that. I told him that I was going to wear whatever I wished, and that he had no right to suggest how I dressed.

This made me very uncomfortable, and I was pleased when he sent me on a job.

When I returned from my job, I rang the doorbell for someone to let me in, but no one answered the door.

I tried again a few more times, but still no response.

Then I realised that he was not going to let me in his house, because of the earlier incident. He was a very traditional Muslim man. His daughter and daughters-in-law had to wear appropriate clothes that covered their entire body and had to have head scarfs. I respected their tradition, as it wasn't far from my Indian tradition, but I was not happy, him trying to change my ways, when my own parents had not objected to how I dressed.

So I never went back to the base after that, apart from when I had to make a payment for the radio. Then, I would just slip an envelope with the money through the letter box.

I still kept in touch with Paz. He was always there to help me, if I had any problem with my car, or if I needed any other help.

We had formed a very good friendship, and he was always obliged to help.

Once, he wanted to treat me to a birthday meal. We went to a lovely restaurant in Piccadilly, in London. After the meal, as we were walking towards his car, he decided that he needed to use the loo. So, he left me waiting on the street, while he looked for a place where he could find a loo. I was so scared, waiting in the street on my own, as a car approached the kerb, and asked me if I was working. I said "No way," and he drove off. He must have got the wrong idea, as I was in a red dress, and red stiletto heels and it didn't help that I was pacing up and down the street, waiting for Paz to appear.

I was wondering where Paz had got to. I wasn't able to move far from the spot, as he might not be able to find me. Then I saw him running towards me, his bunch of keys that he used to hang on his belt jangling, as he ran. He shouted, "Run, quick run, they are coming after me." I had no idea what was going on, but I started running too, towards where his car had been parked, with a lot of difficulty, with my heels on.

We were both out of breath, as we reached the car.

Through his heavy panting he told me what had happened.

He had walked into a club, to use their loo, but as he came out of the cloak room, the doorman stopped him, and asked him for the membership identity, as it was an exclusive club.

Apparently, it was a playboy club. Paz made excuses, and ran out of the club as fast as he could, the doorman chasing after him. I told him about what I had gone through as well, and we laughed, thinking what a pair we were.

Once he had had an offer of having his cars valeted by a man, who was giving him a discount for having a certain amount of cars done. He decided to let me have my car valeted too, for free. Since I had stopped going to the base, I couldn't take my car there and had to book it to be done at my place.

The man came and started the job. I used to park my car in the car park at the back of the house. So, he had to connect his cleaning equipment to my house with a long extension lead. While he was working I offered him a cup of tea. He accepted my offer. In fact, I must have made him about five cups of tea since he was over.

When he was done, I thanked him. He thanked me for the tea, and I jokingly said, "Any time."

In a couple of days' time, there was a knock on my kitchen door. When I went to open it, it was the valet man again. I was surprised to see him, wondering if I was supposed to have paid him, or if he had left something behind.

But all he said was that, he had come over, taking me up on my offer of a cup of tea. I was surprised that he had taken my offer seriously.

Nevertheless, I made us a cup of tea, and chatted about his work and my work. He told me that he only lived a couple of streets away, with his Nan and Granny. His parents were divorced, and they both had new partners, so he preferred living with his Nan and Granny. He also told me that he volunteered as a Special Constable in the Maidenhead police force. He told me that his name was Ian.

When he had left, I rang Paz to tell him about the valet man's visit. He told me that the guy had been asking all about me, wanting to know if I had a partner and asking all kinds of things about me.

So, his visit earlier had been to ask me out.

This did turn into a relationship in the end. It was practical, as he would spend some time with me, and always end up going home to his Nan's, and Granny's.

This was my first relationship since my divorce, so I was very wary and nervous, and wondering how my daughters would take this.

Sirita was alright with it, but Sonal, after a while was not very keen on Ian.

I was also worried about my family finding out. So, this relationship remained a secret.

It was very hard to live a lie. Ian and his family couldn't understand why I was not willing to tell my family about us. But I was just not ready.

Ian was kind enough, hard worker, and a decent man. He would treat me kindly, and respected me. All the things that Arun had lacked. He would take me out for meals, and take me to the seaside in the summer.

He had introduced me to his dad and step mother, who had a young daughter. We would visit them often, and got along very well. I got on very well with his mum too.

I was not ready to tell my family about him, I was afraid that they would not approve of me seeing an English man. Any man in fact.

Soon, he had saved enough to put a deposit on a house. He spent hours working on the property, and was hoping that I would move in with him.

When the time came, I was not happy to move in with him. This property was almost ten miles away from my place. I was worried about my family finding out that I had moved in with a man and my daughters, who might have to change their school, and lose all the friends they had made. They also might not like my living with a man, who was not their dad. I had to take everything into account, like the fact that if our relationship was over for any reason, my girls and I would be homeless. And also that my family would not be able to come and visit me in his house.

I would go and visit Ian in his new house, or he would spend time with me. But I was not willing for us to live together.

My mum had come to stay with me once again and this time she was with me for over a month. So, during her stay, I would see Ian briefly, whenever I had a chance, but most of the time, we would speak on the phone. I had purchased my first mobile phone by now, so it was convenient to speak on the mobile.

After my mum had left he came over to see me. He seemed very distant, and I put his behaviour down to my mum having come to stay with me.

But then he told me that we could not carry on, if I was not willing to tell my family about him. He wanted a partner, he could share his house with and start a family.

But I couldn't give him either of that. So that is when our relationship ended. I was broken hearted, though I knew that I would never change my mind.

We suddenly stopped ringing each other, let alone seeing each other.

I would ring and talk to his step mum and end up sobbing throughout our conversation. She would console me, for that was all she could do.

I was left in a mental state. Some nights I would drive down, near to where Ian lived, park my car away from the house, then walk past his house a few times. A few times I hid in some bushes, opposite his house in a ditch, watching his house. I have no idea why I did this. May be just wanting to have a glance of him in my grieving state. Also wondering if he had found himself a new partner.

Before we had completely stopped talking to each other, when I would say to him that I would ring him that night, he would say that he had a shift to do.

Thinking that he was making excuses, I would drive up to the police station carpark, where all the officers' cars were parked at the back of it, just to make sure that his car was in the carpark and that he was actually working. I became so insecure and possessive.

At times I would drive by his Nan's house to see if he was in or out, getting jealous if his car was not in the drive, wondering where he was.

I was so messed up in my head.

I was so lucky that no one found out, as I might have got into a lot of trouble.

Many weeks passed, and then months passed, and soon I started accepting that it was all over between us.

I decided to involve myself in some sort of activity, and start living my life again. I joined a beginners' swimming class, as I could not swim. I was a bit slow at learning to swim, compared to the other members in the class, but thoroughly enjoyed the classes, and made lots of friends. Unfortunately, I had to give them up when we were made to swim underwater. I just couldn't master that, and would panic as soon as my face went under water. I was told that my breathing techniques were not right, thus not being able to swim underwater.

I also joined a local beginners' class in tennis. I would look forward to my classes, and soon picked up a few skills. That too stopped, when the tennis season was over, and I never went back to them the following season.

I began going to the cinema on my own. I would settle down to watch the movie with some popcorn and a soft drink. I was beginning to like my own company, and my mind was clear of the rubbish and jealousy I had possessed.

I learned that I didn't need anyone, and I became a stronger person.

I even had a go at joining a Salsa dance class, which I thoroughly enjoyed.

In the year 1991, we were hit by recession, and the mini cab company was not doing very well.

There were various new companies that had started up in Maidenhead, so there was a lot of competition going on amongst the cab companies.

I was getting less and less work, may be one job after waiting for at least two to three hours or even longer, each day.

I was getting desperate, and had to think of an alternative job. I started looking for some cleaning jobs, which were hard to come by.

I looked in the local papers for cleaning jobs, and managed to be interviewed by a couple of ladies, but did not get the job.

I even decided to set up my own courier company. I called it Caz Cars Couriers. I had a few cards and leaflets printed, but unfortunately, due to the recession and competition amongst companies, this business did not take off.

After working for at least four years, I finally had to give up the mini cabbing job.

I had the urge to own a jeep, just like the one, one of my uncles used to drive in Uganda.

I talked to Paz about it, and he started searching for a reasonably priced jeep for me. He found me a second hand Suzuki Samurai, soft top, in Army green. I exchanged that with my old car.

I loved my jeep, though my daughters were not keen on it. They would be embarrassed to be seen in it, by their friends.

I had to rely on the government benefits, so I could pay for my housing and day to day living.

I was looking for jobs in the local papers, when I came across a massage course run by a man in Hurley.

I joined his class, and found both the practical and the theory side of the course very interesting. I would go to our local library and borrow books on Anatomy, for my course work. I didn't realise how much study went into a massage course.

In order to improve our practical skills, one of my fellow students, Lesley, and I decided to practise a massage on each other, perhaps once in a week. We would also test each other on the theory side. I would also practise on one of my friends in our neighbourhood, and her five year old daughter, who would appreciate a massage, but then I got to practise my skills.

All the hard work paid off as when we sat our exams, we both passed. Lesley ended up setting up a physiotherapy practice.

I was so proud of myself, achieving an ITEC qualification and receiving a diploma in Anatomy, physiology and massage. Especially looking back on how I was at school in my youth, struggling to pass any of my exams.

I was still struggling to look for a job. Even though I had achieved a new skill, I didn't know how to go about pursuing a career out of it.

Lesley introduced me to a friend of hers who ran a B & B, and was looking for a housekeeper. I had an interview with her, and luckily got the job.

The B & B was a beautiful 16th Century Manor house, converted farm house, situated on perhaps two acres of gardens and a paddock.

The young lady ran the B & B along with her husband, who also ran a wine company.

There were five rooms for hiring in the main house, and chalets, converted from the barn houses. There was also a Jacuzzi and a sauna room, for hire, within the premises.

There was a small stable where they kept a couple of pet donkeys.

My job would be to clean the rooms and chalets, and change the bedding, when needed.

I would also have to do the linen laundry, as well as the ironing.

I soon settled into the job.

There were times, when it was busy, I would help the couple with the breakfast.

I was shown, how the tables should be laid. At first I used to get it wrong, then I drew a sketch of the table setting on a piece of paper and would follow that drawing when laying the table, till I got used to, without looking at it.

Few months into the job, the couple were going on holiday for a week. So, they asked me if I could take care of the B & B during their absence. They ended up hiring a cook for the breakfast to make it easy for me.

I was happy to run the place for a week. They told me that I was welcome to stay in one of the vacant rooms, or go home in the evenings if I preferred.

This started happening more often, when they found that I was capable of coping with their business, by taking bookings, taking payments from customers, checking them in and out along with doing the cleaning of the rooms and chalets.

There were times, when I had to cook breakfast as well, if the cook had not showed up. I used to get very nervous, especially if the guests turned up at the same time for breakfast, trying to remember what they had ordered, but soon picked up speed and efficiency.

My boss's husband had a small five to six seater plane, which he used to often fly from Booker airfield near Marlow, and Wycombe.

He offered to take me on one of his flights. I took Sirita with me. The couple and the two of us had a wonderful experience flying over Oxford and back.

Soon the young couple started their family, and had two beautiful daughters.

They had to hire a permanent cook and another chamber maid, due to being busy with their new extended family and the fact that the B & B was getting very busy. I was earning sufficient money at this job, but needed to earn extra money to be able to pay all my bills so I started selling Tupperware.

I was appointed by a local lady, who trained me and also managed a group of ladies in our area. I was given a kit to start me off, but had to buy items at our demonstration meetings at a discounted price. The Manager would pick all the ladies in our group up and take us to the meetings in her six -seater car. I started doing demonstration parties, starting off with friends in my local area, and then building up to recommendations. Any guest at a party, who was to book a demo party would get a free gift, which encouraged people to book.

I had great fun doing these parties, and this gave me a chance to meet people from all backgrounds.

In order to make the demonstration interesting, I would do some cooking, with the Tupperware items we were selling, and also played games. The one most favoured by the ladies was, trying to place shapes into a Tupperware ball. Whoever finished the quickest would win an item of Tupperware as a gift.

The second one was a board game, I had of catchphrase, where I would flash the cards, and the guests had to write down what catchphrase it represented. Again the winner would win a prize.

I remember my mum going to the Tupperware parties, when we were little, in Uganda. They used to call them kitty parties.

I had to give this up after a year or so, when some of the hostesses had already done a demo a few times, and didn't want to do them anymore. The sales were not very good either, so I was not selling well. I was finding it very hard to find new people to host for.

During this time Paz, whom I had still been in regular contact with since I left my mini cabbing job, rang me to say that the garage where he bought his company cars from were selling a BMW car for a very good price if I would be interested to purchase it. I viewed the car, it was a black soft top, Series 3, Cabriolet.

I fell in love with the car, and started a payment plan with the garage, and part-exchanged the jeep with the garage.

I used to love my BMW, and had great pleasure driving it about.

Mum's new flat

My brothers found that my mum was missing seeing her sister, aunty, and her brother in Wembley, due to the distance between them, and always complained that she felt lonely during the day when my brother and sister-in-law were at work. So, after her staying with my brother for at least fifteen years, they decided to find her a place in London, so that she could easily see her brother and sister's family. They found a one bedroom flat for her in Heston, in Middlesex, which happened to be just a few bus-stops away from my aunty and had a bus stop right opposite her flat with regular buses running all directions. It was a three- way purchase among my mum, Gulab and Ashok. Even though my brothers were nervous to tell our mum of their plan and worried that our mum would think that they were abandoning her, when the time came for her to move into her new flat, she was very excited and started shopping for her new place. She was picking up all the soft furnishings and white goods, looking for the best items, and not settling for any hand me downs.

Her moving to Heston also made it easy for me to go and visit her, as well as my uncle and aunties.

She settled in well, and soon familiarised herself with the area. She would hop on the bus to go shopping and visit her friends, and go see her doctors, without anyone having to take her. She even joined a ladies' group, where they would meet and share food, cooked by each individual.

This made our family very happy, to see our mum settled and happy, and especially her being independent.

We would have a big family gathering on her birthdays, either at her flat, or in a restaurant, that my brothers would arrange, so as to make her know that we all cared for her and loved her. She definitely loved all the attention.

Whenever I was to go visit her she would have a feast ready of her delicious cooking. She would do that no matter who visited her. I learned a lot of cooking skills from her, watching her cook.

She loved having company. If ever I told her that I was to visit her, she would prepare the food, and then sit by the window for hours, looking out and waiting for me to arrive.

I started visiting her regularly, taking her shopping or to visit relatives and friends.

Working at the Salon

Though I was doing well at the Manor House, I was still hoping to practise my massage.

I found an advert in the local paper for a room to rent. It had been advertised by a lady called Anja who ran a Nail Manicure salon situated by the river in Maidenhead. She settled for a small fee, to be paid weekly, so I set up my massage practice from her salon.

It was a bit slow going, but I would only go to the salon if I had appointments.

Next door to my room, a young lady called Tammy ran her hairdressing shop.

Then there were a few other nail technicians in the main room working for Anja.

Just a couple of months into working at the salon, we had to abandon the premises, due to a building project plan coming into place, at the premises.

The lady I rented the room from moved to new premises in White Waltham, and took all her nail technicians with her, as well as the hairdresser. I was given a choice to leave or rent a room from her again, and I decided to take her up on her offer.

I started advertising my business in the local papers, and soon started picking up customers. I named my business 'Relax' and had some business cards and pamphlets printed.

I would normally go in to work if I had bookings, otherwise I would stay at home, till I got a call, and then drive to work, which was only 10 minutes away.

I got to know the rest of the nail technicians at the salon, and soon we started going out for drinks and meals after work, and formed a little group of friends. I had a great social life with them.

There was Maria, Cecelia and Julie, who were the nail technicians, who worked for Anja, whereas Tammy rented out a room for her saloon, like myself, from her.

We soon made plans to go on holiday together. I had never been abroad, since my trip to India with my ex-husband. So, I was not too sure if I would join them. Then, as they were making plans to maybe go to Egypt I was tempted to join them, for I had always been fascinated by Egyptian history and dreamt of going there one day, and this gave me an opportunity to fulfil my dream. We had stopped for one night at a hotel in Cairo, during our travels from Uganda when we first came to England. It had only been an overnight stay. So, we had not been able to do any sightseeing or see the great pyramids we had heard of.

Sonal had settled in her home and Sirita too had left school and was in a job. She had turned sixteen. So, I did not have to worry about leaving the girls behind.

As we were making our last- minute plans to go on a holiday, Anja was not happy for all of us to be absent from work at the same time. But we had already made our minds up, and went ahead with booking our holiday.

This made things awkward between our boss and us, and the atmosphere in the salon went completely sour.

On our return, back from Egypt, Anja had laid down certain strict rules for her girls which created a bit of a conflict among all of us.

Soon, Julie and Maria decided to give their notice in, and went to work as self-employed. Tammy, too followed and set up her hairdressing business.

Cecelia was the only one who remained for a while, but then she too left.

Anja had to recruit some new staff.

I had carried on with my massage business, till I was offered an opportunity to work from the Berkshire Polo Club, near Ascot. One of my customers owned the Polo Club, and believed that I could earn a lot of money, if some of the Polo players were to become my customers.

I took up this opportunity, left Anja's salon and set up my business from a barn that had to be converted into a salon.

I found that I had to spend a lot of my own money, to make the place look decent enough. I bought some plants and lightings, and also had to purchase some heaters than ran on gas bottles, as the barn was very cold. These gas bottles forever needed replacing, for I had to keep them running till I left for the day. The barn roof was so high up, that all the heat would escape upwards.

I would have a few previous customers that would still come to my new place, but most of them were not prepared to come due to the distance.

At the old place, Anja would encourage her clients to have a trial massage by me, and soon they would become my regulars. With that and the advertisement in the local papers I had been doing well, but that soon changed at the Polo Club.

I found that I was paying out more rent than I was earning. The promise of the Polo Players, using my salon was not kept by the owner. He actually wanted me to mingle with the crowd when the polo matches took place, and try and promote my business, but it was not practical for me to do so, for the grounds and the polo pitches were often wet and muddy, and I would not be dressed appropriately for the conditions.

I carried on still, and thought that I would let the holiday be over, before taking any steps. I didn't know where else to take my business.

Our Holiday in Egypt

Before having left Anja's salon, we had booked a holiday for Luxor in Egypt. There were four of us who planned to go. Maria, Tammy, Julia and myself. I was so excited, and was behaving like a kid at the airport, jumping up and down in excitement.

As we landed at Luxor Airport and left the terminal, there was a sudden waft of smell in the air. It smelt, warm and kind of spicy. I could tell that we were in a different country.

Our hotel was situated near the Nile, where there were rows of cruise boats docked, bobbing up and down, waiting to take people on their Nile cruises. There was a strong smell coming from the Nile, of the diesel fuel, which laced the waters with the escaping fuel, displaying rainbow colours in the water. To start off our holiday, we booked a trip to the famous Karnak Temple in Luxor. The beautiful temple was built about 2,000 years ago, dated from 2055 BC to around 100 AD. It was a great pleasure walking through the ruins, amongst pylons and huge pillars and the giant columns depicting the stories about the Pharoahs and the kings and the gods, in the form of carvings and hieroglyphics.

There was also an 80- feet Obelisk that was over 3,000 years old, placed at the entrance of the temple.

Our next excursion was to the Valley of the Kings and Queens, where lay most of the tombs of the great Pharoahs, Kings and Queens. These were huge underground tombs, where the kings' burial chambers were. The walls in these tombs were painted brightly with depictions and hieroglyphics, telling stories about the king. After his death, the king's embalmed and mummified body would be laid in a sarcophagus, inside these tombs with all his belongings that would serve him in his afterlife.

His viscera would be placed in canopic jars, each jar carrying a specific organ. These were also placed in the tombs.

We were shown the inside of a few famous tombs, and given a commentary and the story about each tomb, by a guide.

We were very lucky to be able to go into the chambers of the famous boy King Tutankhamun.

The boy king whose intact tomb was discovered by the Egyptologist Howard Carter in 1922. Most of the tombs had been looted of all their precious possessions by robbers, but Tutankhamun's was full of treasures and belongings that had been placed in his tomb for his afterlife.

At the Valley of the Queens, we visited the temple of the Queen Hatshepsut. The temple of magnificent architecture was constructed in 1479 BC on her orders. The vast temple located in Upper Egypt, was basking in the hot sun in its glory. Visiting it was a great experience.

We were on an excursion to Dendera which was on a boat. There was music playing, and everyone was enjoying the food and drinks provided. We got off the boat at the location of the Dendera Temple Complex. A very well-preserved temple which also contained the temple of Hathor, the goddess of the sky, women and fertility. She is often depicted as a goddess with cow's horns, a red sun disk on her head. After the sightseeing, we boarded the boat again which was to bring us back to the hotel.

Strangely enough there was no music being played this time. Even though it was getting dark, there were only a few lights on, on the boat. When we docked at the river bank, we had our hotel reps waiting for us. They rushed us on board a mini bus, and as we pulled away, we were told that there had been some trouble, and we had to be taken back to the hotel, and were advised not to leave the hotel.

We soon learned that there had been a mass shooting at the Temple of Queen Hatshepsut, at the Valley of the Queens, where we had been the previous day. We considered ourselves lucky that we had not visited the temple on the day of the shootings.

There were almost 62 people killed by Islamic terrorists. They had been hiding in the mountains, and started the massacre, not caring whom they killed. The dead were mostly tourists. This massacre happened on 17th November 1997.

We realised why the boat had not been lit up or any music played. They had to keep a low key, as it had to be made look like a local boat, in case there were terrorists in hiding, and were prepared to shoot at the tourists

We were told that we had to leave the country the next day. We were not happy to do so as we were into the third day of our holiday. But unfortunately, we had no choice but to leave for home the next day, driven to the airport under armed guard.

As we landed back home, friends and family were pleased to see us come back safe and sound.

The Gambia

On our return, we decided to try and get compensation from the travel agents, whom we had booked our holiday to Egypt with.

Each of us was compensated with £300 each, towards the unfortunate ordeal we had to go through. I was happy to receive the £300, but my friends thought that this amount was not enough, so decided to ask for more money.

To our surprise, the Travel agents made us another offer of picking a holiday of our choice for up to the cost of £300, to be had, on top of the money already received.

We began looking through holiday brochures, for yet another holiday.

We all settled for a holiday in the Gambia, in West Africa. Soon the date was set, and the four of us were off to the Gambia.

We landed at the Banjul Airport, and were then driven to our hotel, as the night set in.

We were led to our apartment, almost in the dark, as there were only a few lights on, at the complex. We dragged our suitcases on the paths leading to our apartment.

It was very basic, but clean enough. We were to share a large room, consisting of four single beds.

After unpacking, we decided to go for a drink at the bar. The staff members led us towards a little hut, which was a bar by the swimming pool. We had a drink at this bar, then Tammy asked the barman, where the proper bar was. To this he replied that this was the Hotel bar.

We started wondering what sort of hotel we had landed at, with a tiny little bar, run from a hut.

When we had settled back in our room, we found that the African heat was unbearable, and we could not sleep. We asked for some air-conditioning, which they kindly provided us with.

As the room started cooling, we started feeling cold. In the middle of the night, we were whispering to each other that we were too cold, now that the air-conditioning was on. We complained amongst ourselves, and giggled away as we shivered under our sheets.

In the morning light, we went for a walk around the complex, and found it to be basic.

We asked to be moved into another room, but as we were shown into the room, it turned out to be just as basic as the first one, so we decided not to make any fuss.

We went out for a walk on the beach on the coast of the Atlantic, just yards away from the hotel complex, and were greeted by the locals. The vendors tried selling us their goods, like sunglasses, African jewellery and T-shirts.

We set out into the Bangul town, to look for somewhere to eat.

As we walked through the streets, the memories of my life in Kampala flooded back in my mind. I could smell the African air, I was familiar with.

We would go out shopping, and look for places to eat each day.

There were some little shops just outside of the hotel complex , one of them being a hairdresser's, where Tammy had her hair braided. I too had a couple of braids with beads dangling from them on both sides of my head, as I did not want my whole head braided.

Then there was the gift shop selling African carvings and jewellery, and next to it was a telephone shop, where the tourists went to make phone calls and send faxes.

Every evening, when we would return from our days out, we would pass by the lads who owned the shops, who would be gathered by the shops and would be playing Reggae music and the African drums.

They told us of a night club in town.

We asked Maria, the hairdresser, if they might be able to take us there.

We took them up on their offer one night, as they stressed that it would be a bit dangerous, for us to go on our own without a chaperone. They looked after us, and brought us back safely.

We booked an excursion to visit the Juffureh village, which is famous of its history of the slave trade. This is where Kunta Kinte was enslaved. His story was made into a book, followed by a series, shown on the television, called "Roots".

We were taken to the Museum, where all the slave movement memorabilia were displayed, like shackles, handcuffs, pistols and ammunition that would have been used during the slave trade.

We were taken into a huge hut, where we were introduced to, what we were told was Kunta Kinte's family. How much of that was true, we weren't sure.

The village was run, just like it would have been centuries ago. The local women were seen pounding their grains using large wooden mortar and pestles, often two women taking turns to pound the grain, whilst singing, dressed in their vibrant, colourful, African outfits.

We also had a trip to city of Serekunda, where we walked through the markets, after which we went to visit the Kachikally, where the crocodile pool was located. People were actually touching the tamed crocodiles, but I stayed yards away from them and had a photo taken.

We had soon got accustomed to the hotel, and found that all the staff, and the people around us were very friendly, and keen to help. We didn't care that the bar was basic, it was the bar tenders, who were amazing, and entertained us.

We were invited to join the rest of the holidaymakers to a barbecue, run by the complex. We joined the party, and sampled the African food which was delicious.

While the party was going on Maria was having her hair braided, at the hairdresser's by the complex, so we were taking turns, taking plates of food for her, so that she did not miss out on the delicious African food.

We had had yet another great holiday.

As we were waiting for our flight back at the airport, we came across a lady who did a bit of charity work for the local schools in the Gambia.

Tammy and Maria were keen to help her, so later on after coming back home, they planned another trip to the Gambia, and were given a place to stay, in return for helping with a bit of painting at a school. They also took with them books, pens and pencils for the poor students.

The two of them had a great time staying in the Gambia, and had loads of interesting stories to tell us on their return.

Working at the Mars Chocolate factory

I went back to work, but was worried about the business, as I could not survive on the money I was earning.

Then a customer of mine mentioned that the Mars Confectionery Factory in Slough were recruiting some Temps, and that if I didn't mind working in a factory, should try applying for a job there.

I managed to find out more about the vacancy and turned up at the recruiting Agency to apply for the job.

I soon got confirmation that my application was successful, and was asked to attend the medical and the training course.

I had to go through various tests before I could start work, like an eye test, hearing test.

After the training, I had to sit a written test.

I managed to pass all the tests and was given the job as a Picker/Packer, on the conveyor belts.

I gave in my notice at the Polo Club, without any regret, and looked forward to my new job, in a chocolate factory.

The job entailed night shifts and day shifts. The rota would consist of ten hours of perhaps three day shifts and four night shifts and time off in between, and vice versa.

My first shift happened to be a night shift.

I was given a locker and photo identity card, which had to be worn at all times. There were white uniforms of all sizes in the locker room, and I had to change into the whites, along with a hard hat, with my hair covered in a blue hair net, and steel toed shoes, before entering the factory's departments.

My line manager showed me, along with a few other new recruits to a conveyor belt that had chocolates being transported on their way to be wrapped. Our job was to pick any misshapen or damaged sweets off the belt and drop them in some bins, which could then be recycled and re-processed.

We were given half an hour for our tea break, and an hour for a dinner break after every two hours of working which made it easy to work a night shift.

I soon made friends and was thoroughly enjoying my job.

Some of the workers would play pranks on the new comers by sticking a chocolate wrapper, held by sticky tape on back of their hats. Unaware, they would walk around with it, till someone alerted them.

I was once a victim of such a prank. I had a wrapper stuck to the back of my hat, at the end of the shift. I walked to the locker room unaware, and wondered why everyone passing by smiled at me. Most probably giggling behind my back. I noticed it when I took my hat off.

I started brushing my hand over my hat, after someone had just passed behind me, in case they had played a prank on me again.

After a few months working on this line, I was shifted to a different plant of the factory.

There were two plants of the same factory, one was at Dundee Road and one at Liverpool Road, on the Trading Estate in Slough. Being a Temp, I had chances of being moved to either of these plants, when and where needed.

By this time The Mars Company had introduced 12-hour shifts.

I was moved to the Medicated department which was at Liverpool Road, where the menthol sweets, Tunes and Lockets were manufactured. My job was to pack the sweets into boxes and also packing the packed boxes into cases. To begin with, I was a bit slow with the packing, which was not good, for if the boxes piled up, the machines would automatically stop, and this would mean that the production would come to a halt. Some of my colleagues would have to give me a helping hand, till the lines were cleared. But soon I picked up speed and managed to carry on without any help.

Soon, more Temps were recruited into our department, so we would take turns to take over packing, while one of us was on a break. I was paired up with a young lad called Jag.

We had a fantastic manager, who would encourage us to learn different skills on the line. The permanent staff would show us how to run the wrapping machines which were called TF2's. Once we had mastered that we were also encouraged to dismantle the machines and put them back together, with the guidance of the permanent staff whenever the lines were down, and it was time for maintenance and cleaning.

We soon mastered that too.

The complicated maintenance was always carried out by the skilled Maintenance staff.

The trained Temps would run the department by themselves if the permanent staff were at a meeting. Our nice manager would walk past, and be proud of us working so hard.

We became a great team.

There was a young permanent worker, called Alan, who was always up to mischief. He would pick up one of the ladies and throw them into the skip that was full of waste wrapping paper.

Then he would watch them struggling to come out of the skip. He was forever playing pranks with the ladies. I too had been thrown into the skip, many a time.

Our manager had spoken to the Temping agency Manager, about my performance in his department and the enthusiasm I had shown at learning new skills.

So, I was called over for a meeting with him and offered a job as a team leader. This job would coincide with my daily job.

I was elated hearing the news and accepted the offer.

Upon becoming a team leader, my pay went up. I was given a sticker with 'Team Leader' on it, to be placed next to my name on the hard hat. I was given a bleeper, in order for me to contact the managers, maintenance staff or any other member of the company, who had a bleeper.

My job entailed making sure that all the Temp staff due to work on the day had clocked in on time. If there were any absent members, I would first of all ring them, to make sure that they were on their way. If not, than I had to inform the different line managers of their absence, and to find out if they needed a replacement, during the managers' meetings which were held daily, before a takeover from the previous shift.

There would be some Temps come in as standby's so it would be my job to allocate them to the vacant positions. At this point it was reasonable to place the appropriately skilled Temp to the available job. There were various other duties, like removing the clock cards in the middle of the shift and replacing them for the following shift. I thoroughly enjoyed the extra duties I was given.

Some times during my breaks, I would sit in the locker room and read Philippa Gregory books. I would be so engrossed in the book and forget what time it was. So, I started setting the alarm on my phone to alert me. At times, if I had no books at hand, I would play the snake game on my Motorola phone.

Some of us had also formed a card playing group. Since we were in different departments, we would try and arrange to go on the same breaks, so that we could play Gin Rummy in the Canteen.

Sonal

Sonal had sat her GCSC exams, and was not up for furthering her studies. So, she found herself a job.

She would go out with her friends to parties, and sometimes had sleep overs. Most of her friends lived within our neighbourhood and their parents were known to me. So, I didn't mind her having sleepovers. Sometimes her friends would come for a sleepover at my place. They would all set up their beds on the floor in our through-lounge, and play music, giggle like teenagers do, and enjoy themselves.

There was a time, when one evening, she went out with her friends and didn't return home. She had not arranged a sleepover. It was getting late, so I started ringing around her friends, to find out who she was with. They all said that she had been with the group of friends at the pub, but had left before they did. After having contacted every source, where she could have been, I started panicking as it got very late in the night.

I had to ring the police, telling them that my daughter had gone missing. They came to the house to take a statement and asked for her recent photo. I was getting hysterical and was having all sorts of negative thoughts as to what might have happened to her.

I ended up ringing my sister for her support. She turned up, with my brother-in-law and their kids, who had been picked up from their beds, the sleepy heads still in their pyjamas.

We all wanted desperately for any information from the police.

Then, early hours of the morning, they knocked on the door. I rushed to open it. There she was, accompanied by two police officers. Sonal had been found by the police.

I was elated, though I wanted to shout at her. I was just happy that she had been returned, safely home.

She could not understand what the panic and fuss was all about. She said that she was old enough to look after herself.

Apparently, she had gone to the pub with her friends, where she met a young man she had taken a fancy to. She ended up going off with him to his flat, and none of her friends knew where he lived.

Panic over for now, she carried on seeing her young man, Richard, who shared a house with some friends. He had arrived in the area to find work, all the way from Sunderland, where his family lived.

Not long after meeting Richard, Sonal announced that she had fallen pregnant.

I was so shocked and was not prepared to digest the news. I shouted at both her and Richard, like mothers do, when in a panic state.

Richard reassured me that he would stick by Sonal and care for her.

There was nothing else I could do, but let the circumstances take their course.

I was dreading telling my family the news, which I couldn't keep from them, as they would eventually find out. I rang my brother, Gulab, to give him the news, as my mum was staying with him at the time, before her move, and I hoped that he would speak to my mum, so that I wouldn't have to.

As I broke the news to him, his first words were, "Congratulations! You are going to be a grandmother!"

My reaction was, "Phew", and I took a long breath. He had taken the news without judgement.

My mum also went along with the fact, and didn't scold me or Sonal, as I worried that she would give us a stern telling off.

Sonal started flourishing in her pregnancy, and I too started looking forward to her baby.

Just before the birth of their baby, Sonal and Richard moved out, and started renting a house in Slough.

I got a call from Richard, to say that Sonal had started her contractions, and had been taken to hospital.

When I got there, she was being taken to the delivery room. Upon seeing her in pain and in labour, I just went all hot and felt nauseous and thought that I was going to faint. Richard walked me out of the hospital, and left me out there in the fresh air, to recover. By the time I felt that I could go back in, Sonal had already given birth to a baby girl.

My beautiful granddaughter, Amie Lauren Townsend, was born on 27th October 1996. I was a very proud Nani to be blessed with a beautiful granddaughter, and loved and enjoyed the years of her growing up.

When Sonal was still in hospital, in the recovery room after the birth of Amie, I had just gone to the hospital shop to get some snacks, when a couple, who looked a bit lost, asked me where the Maternity ward was. I told them to follow me in the lift, as I was going there too.

When we walked towards the ward, they walked towards Sonal's bed.

It so happened that they were Richard's parents.

I had never met them before, as they lived in Sunderland, and had specially come over to see Baby Amie.

Both Sonal and Richard were great parents to Amie, and I was very proud of them.

Sirita in her teens

When Sirita finished her secondary schooling, she too decided to start work. Her starting to earn money, meant that her Child Benefit stopped, and a few other benefits I was getting help with due to a low income stopped too.

She would go to work weekdays then hang around with her school friends at weekends. Her best friend lived in Bourne End, so she found herself a job in that area. She also helped clean the donkey stables at Sheep House Manor, where I used to work, in order to earn a few pounds.

Another job she did was after school cleaning, at a private school in Maidenhead.

She started taking driving lessons, and bought a car, hoping that she would drive it after passing her driving test.

I would hardly see her, for she would be out with her friends, or I would be on my night shift.

I came home after 7pm one evening, after the morning shift. I had taken her car to work and on my return, parked it in the carpark at the back of the house.

I was settling in for bed that night, when I heard her come in through the backdoor. She did not stop to come up and see me, and within minutes she had gone out again. I fell asleep, but was woken up from my sleep, when she entered my bedroom crying and panicking.

When I asked her what the matter was, she told me that she had taken the car and smashed it into a stationary car, not far from where we lived.

I too panicked and quickly changed out of my night clothes, and we both walked up to the place where she had had the accident. It was gone midnight and the place was very quiet and there was hardly a soul about. I tried to drive the car away from the scene, but the front tyre had buckled into the other car and would not budge.

She was getting hysterical, so not being able to release the car, we ran back home, not knowing what to do next. Like any parent would like to protect their child, I rang the Police and told them that our car had been stolen. They took all the details, and said that they would ring me if they found it.

We could hardly sleep that night, then early hours of the morning, I told her that I would have to tell the police the truth, for we would get into trouble for lying. She said that she was also thinking about telling the police the truth.

Not long after, there was a knock on the door, and a couple of policemen at the door. I let them in and before they said anything, I told them that it was my daughter who had had the accident, and that the car had not been stolen.

One of the officers, said that they knew all along, as Sirita had been seen fleeing the scene by some neighbours, where the crash had occurred, and had in fact come over to arrest her for falsely giving information, and as we had come out with the truth, before they could charge us, I had been pardoned, but Sirita had to spend a night in custody, and have a statement taken from her.

Both of us had our profile pictures taken, as well as fingerprints.

She was released the next day, and her licence was revoked for a year.

She went on to buy another car from some friends. As she was unable to drive it, I started driving it, and sold my BMW, as we were not able to run two cars, and I was also finding it hard to maintain the cost of running the BMW.

After her disqualification was up, she passed her driving test and was able to drive her car and became very independent.

I was very angry with her, but then I remembered the time when I was more or less her age, I had driven, many a time, the car I had gone and bought, without a licence and insurance.

I was just lucky that I had not been caught or had an accident.

My parents would never have spared me.

There had been another incident, where she had gone to a night club, run for young teenagers, at the Maidenhead's leisure centre, called Escapades.

I got a call from the centre, telling me that I had to come and collect my daughter, who had been intoxicated.

I rushed to go collect her, and she was brought out on a wheel chair by the staff. She would not respond to me, when I asked her, if she had had a drink, or if her drink had been spiked.

I was so embarrassed, when I noticed that the staff member who had wheeled her out on the wheelchair happened to be my Swimming teacher.

I have never found out, to this date, what had happened that evening.

New beginning for Sonal

Soon Sonal and Richard were able to put a deposit down on a flat in Slough and moved in with their first born, Amie. Richard had come into some money from an inheritance from his Grandmother, which helped them towards the purchase of their property.

Once they were settled in their new flat, Sonal and Richard made plans to get married.

I was not able to give them a lavish wedding, but with the help of my brother, Gulab, and my mum gifting me some money, was able to at least give them a decent wedding.

We went to a local wedding dress shop to browse and get ideas for a wedding dress. Trying on a few dresses and fell in love with one of the dresses. I ended up hiring it for her. We also picked the bridesmaid dresses, for Sirita and one of Sonal's best friends.

Little Amie too had a beautiful sheer tulle bridesmaid dress in white. She looked like an angel.

In my eyes, she was the most beautiful girl in the world.

Sonal wanted to wear white gold on her wedding so I exchanged some gold bangles for a set of white gold necklace and pearl earrings.

I even managed to hire a Limousine, from a colleague in the Mars factory, whose family ran a business of hiring luxury cars for very reasonable rates.

On her wedding day, we arrived in style at the Registry Office, followed by a Reception which was held at a church hall in Wexham.

I managed to get wine bottles for a cheap price from my boss at the Sheep House Manor, from his wine warehouse. The food was ordered from a catering company.

On the morning of the wedding, the bride-to- be and the rest of us had our hair done. Maria had painted my nails a few days earlier. Which to this date, she has regularly done.

It was not a very big wedding, with my brothers and sisters-in-law, my sister and her family, Richards's parents and his brother's family and a few of Sonal's and Richard's friends.

I also had a few of my neighbourhood friends, Tammy, and Maria attend their wedding.

The wedding went very well, the newlyweds danced the night away to their favourite music, and Amie ran around in her beautiful dress, fussed over by everyone.

The Nile Cruise

Maria was planning going back to Egypt on a Nile Cruise in order to celebrate her sister's birthday. She had previously done such a cruise, and highly recommended the experience. Once again I was tempted to join them. So, we made plans to go. It was just the three of us this time.

We landed in Luxor, and were taken to the banks of the Nile in a mini bus, where a large number of boats were docked. We were dropped at the Cruise Boat named "King Tut". As we were led to our cabin, we passed the foyer, and noticed a huge golden mask of King Tut, displayed in the Reception. There were other elaborate, ornate furniture and finery displayed all over the foyer entrance.

Our cabin, which the three of us shared, too was very modern and very well furnished.

We went to dine in the evening, in a luxurious dining room, where lunch, breakfast and dinner would also be served, greeted by smartly dressed waiters. The buffet was laid out in large silver servers, containing various Egyptian Cuisine. We were so spoilt for choice, we tried every bit of food that took our fancy. My favourite turned out to be Falafel's which I had never tried before. I loved them so much, that I asked the chef to give me the recipe.

We were given an itinerary for the week. We were to visit various temples and sites, during our cruise, and were to be accompanied by a guide, to all the sites, for the duration of our stay on the boat. On our first night the boat started sailing, and we went up on the deck to admire the beautiful views.

In the morning, when we woke up, we had already docked in a place called Edfu. After breakfast, we went to see the Temple of Edfu, which is a temple built to honour Horus, the falcon-headed god of war.

Our second stop was in Kom Ombo another temple honoured to Horus as the Crocodile God, Sobek, where we saw mummified crocodiles.

We made friends with the rest of the passengers and often sat in groups and socialised with them.

There was a particular old couple, whom we would join for a game of cards most evenings. We all normally sat at the same dining table, thus formed our group of friends.

Our Guide was very friendly and likeable by everyone. He happened to be a Coptic Christian.

The next stop was to visit the Temple of Philae, the temple of the goddess Isis, Osiris and Horus, situated on the island of Philae, which is downstream of Aswan Dam and Lake Nasser.

Lake Nasser happens to be the largest man-made lake, which was created as a result of the creation of the Aswan High dam, across the Nile. The construction was started in 1958 and completed in 1971. In order to sail to Aswan, we had to go through the Esna lock, which was just wide enough, for the cruise boats to go through. The Captains of the boats would sail through the lock with great skill and precision.

The boat docked at Aswan, and we were able to visit both the Upper and the Lower Aswan Dam. It was amazing to hear of the history of the building of these two dams.

The last stop was in Nubia. The Nubians were of an African descent. We had a walk around, buying gifts from vendors, till it was time to head back to our boat, and we sailed back to Luxor, stopping at the Botanical gardens of Kitchener's Island. This was on the small island on the River Nile, given to Lord Horacio Kitchener, who had turned it into a Botanical Garden.

Back in Luxor, we visited the Karnak Temple. This temple dates back from 2055 BC to around 100AD. It was built as a cult temple, dedicated to Amun, the God of Sun and Air, Mut, the mother goddess and Khonsu, who was the son of Mut. This was a vast temple, with columns after columns of the gods depicted on them, in the form of carvings telling stories of gods.

Maria and I decided to do a hot air balloon ride, the day before our last day on the Nile Cruise, while her sister planned to visit the Abu Simbel Temple.

We had to set out early hours of the morning, so that we could see the beautiful sunrise. We were taken to the site of the Hot air Balloon, on a small boat, where we were served breakfast and tea.

We jumped into the basket, and the pilot took off gently, till we reached high up in the sky. We witnessed the most amazing sunrise from the Balloon - the giant star, its red and orange glint reflecting in the waters of the Nile.

The Balloon was travelling gently over the Nile, from where we had the aerial view of the Karnak Temple, and all the boats lined up on the banks of the Nile. A spectacular bird's eye view.

As we got higher, and higher we noticed some black objects moving, what appeared to be a swarm of black ants?

When we asked the pilot what these objects were, he started descending, so we could have a good look for ourselves what we were looking at. Amazingly, the black objects happened to be a group of women in their black robes, heading to a funeral, all gathering at a particular house.

We must have been so high up in the sky that they were like black dots, moving.

As we descended, we could see people sleeping in their beds, on their terraces. We could see farmers tending to their farms.

The pilot was not getting permission to land anywhere, so to our advantage, he kept on flying till we landed on a farm. As we landed the huge canvas of the Balloon covered us up, and the farmers had to come and release us, and help us out.

I found that to be an amazing experience I would never forget.

On the day of Maria's sister's birthday, we started having drinks on the deck, with some snacks we had purchased, but the party ended up in our Tour Guide's Cabin. There were about fifteen of us all cramped into the little cabin, yet we had a great party, singing and drinking, fanning ourselves from the heat in the cabin, with whatever suitable item we could get hold of.

This holiday was yet another amazing experience.

Back to work

It was back to work after a great holiday in Egypt. I had fallen in love with the place. Every experience we had in Egypt was brilliant. I loved the culture, the history, the food and the hospitality of the Egyptians.

I was busy packing away in the packing area when I noticed that one of the boxes of the Tunes sweets had a white piece of paper, visible through the cellophane wrapping. I placed the box amongst the other reject boxes.

I noticed that Jag had been hovering around me. When there was a bit of a break from packing, I started undoing the reject boxes, which would have to be re-fed through the wrapping machine. Jag stood next to me, chatting away. When I got to the box with the white paper, he asked me what that might be, before I disposed of it in the bin. I unfolded the piece of paper, and found a note on it. It read, "Are you free to go out with me?"

I asked Jag if he knew who had sent this, and if it was meant for me. He shrugged his shoulders and soon disappeared. I could sense that he was up to no good.

Later, when I went past the wrapping room, everyone seemed to smile at me like they knew, about the prank, but no one would tell me who it was.

I guessed it was the young lad, Alan, who always played pranks on the ladies.

I was wrong, as I soon found out that there was a man who worked in the department, next to the packing bay who had sent the note. He had gone over to the wrapping room, and slipped the note in one of the boxes, which would have travelled all the way from the packing area to the wrapping room, on the belts, for me to find, and had asked Jag to make sure that I read it.

I did not respond to the note, for when I saw this man, he seemed much older than me, and I was not interested in him at all. Over the weeks, he would go past and try and make small chat with me.

I soon got to know him, and found that he was a kind person, always willing to help people out in the department.

He told me that he was a single parent with a teenage son. He had come to England from Kenya. So, I felt that we had something in common. We became good friends, and he once took me out on a drive in his car, after work. I noticed that he had an Indian god idol placed on his dashboard. This made me believe that he was a Hindu, like me. He had given himself an English name, so I was never sure what religion he practised. He was always kind enough to clean my car which would be parked in the factory carpark during winter time, of the frost or snow, before I got to it, after a shift. I thought that to be very considerate of him.

Soon he introduced me to his son, and his sister, and her family. They welcomed me with open arms and were very nice to me.

He took me and my granddaughter Amie, along with his son to a few Theme Parks, and would spoil Amie with ice cream and food, and if she got tired, he would carry her on his shoulders.

He would shower me with gifts, and occasionally cook for me at his place.

Soon I introduced him to Sirita, Sonal and Richard.

They too seemed okay with him and his son.

I even took him to one of my nieces' wedding, where all my family met him.

He treated me and Amie to a day at Alton Towers, as well as Thorpe Park. Then he took me on a holiday to the Spanish Island of Ibiza, along with his son, who was about fourteen years of age at that time. We had a great week's holiday. I couldn't thank him enough for his kindness.

I invited him and his son to join my girls, Richard and Amie for a Christmas meal, a lovely traditional dinner. We all played games and had a great laugh, and I found him to be getting on so well with my family.

The year went by, but soon I noticed a change in his behaviour. He would not see me or ring me as often as he used to. He would be okay at work with me, but outside of work, his behaviour changed.

When Christmas approached, again I invited him and his son over for a meal. This time it was only going to be Sirita and myself present at home.

He told me on the phone, not to cook, as he was going to treat us.

When he arrived, he had brought with him an Indian takeaway. I didn't seem to mind, but Sirita was annoyed that she could not have a traditional Christmas dinner, which had been an ongoing tradition for years, and to which she had been looking forward so much.

The next day he told me that the reason for not having a Christmas dinner was, that he did not believe in Christmas, and that he wanted to bring up his son as a Muslim.

This really shocked me. He had never disclosed that he was a practising Muslim. He and his son had happily enjoyed the Christmas meal the previous year.

I could not see why he would have Indian God idols in his car, and yet practise Islam.

The next time I visited his house, he showed me a copy of the Koran, and told me that his son was very keen on practising Islam.

I had to give him the benefit of doubt, and accepted his decision.

If ever, I asked him if I could go and see him, he would have an excuse that he was with his family.

I caught him with his lies, when once I had given him a ring to see if I could go and see him, as I was not far from his home, and would be going past his house he told me that he was at his mum's house. But when I drove by, I saw him hanging around with a group of lads, outside his house. This made me realise that he no longer wanted to see me.

One day, a colleague of mine asked me if I was no longer seeing him.

I didn't wish to discuss about whatever was going on, and I said that I was still with him. To this, she told me that a new Temp had started working in his department and that in the locker room, she had been showing everyone a gift that had been presented to her by him.

I was shocked to hear that, as she was a young teenager, old enough to be his daughter. I had spoken to her many times, as I was her team leader. I found that she was made to believe that I had finished the relationship months ago.

When I approached him and asked him about the young girl he just denied it. Then when I asked him about the gifts he had been giving her, he said that he liked giving gifts to people he was fond of.

That just did it for me. I turned away from him without a word, and from that day onwards, I just ignored him. If he walked past me, I would not acknowledge him, like he didn't even exist.

He was out of my life as fast as he had entered it.

When I first met him, he had told me that he had been married to an English lady. They had been divorced. He also said how he had stopped his ex-wife from seeing her son, because of the disagreements they had about how he should have been raised.

He told me that she would not acknowledge him, if ever she bumped into him.

It all made sense to me now, for I was doing the same.

I just got him out of my head, and actually was glad it was all over. For I didn't like the way he was playing games with me. I had gone through a lot with Arun, I was not going to let another man control my life again.

I started enjoying life with my friends. We would go to night clubs and had a very full social life.

When my friend Tammy turned 30, we planned to go to Egypt again, to celebrate her birthday. But this time we went to Cairo.

CAIRO

We stayed at a beautiful hotel very near to the Great Pyramids of Giza. In fact, when we stood on the balcony of the hotel, we could see the tops of the Pyramids. At the start of our holiday we set out to explore the area. We found that we could easily walk to the site where the Pyramids were, and had a great time walking around in the hot sun and the hot sand, amongst some camels, whose owners were encouraging us to have a ride on them. We booked ourselves to go visit the inside of the Pyramid. That happened to be an amazing experience. Once inside the Pyramid, we walked up a very narrow shaft, crouching as it got narrower, till we got right to the top. We entered a chamber where stood a sarcophagus. It was empty, but some people were lying in them to have a picture taken.

There was a small vent at the top of the chamber that let in a beam of sunlight into the dark chamber. There was an eerie feeling standing in this chamber. We could not stay there long for lack of oxygen and fresh air. Once out of the Pyramid, we sat on a wall, in full view of the fantastic, Great Sphinx of Giza, munching on the Starburst sweets I had purchased at the Mars shop.

The next day, we decided to take a taxi from outside of our hotel, to take us sightseeing. The driver, Hussain took us to the souk market and to the Mohammed Ali mosque. We walked through the alleys of the market, where there was a sweet and mild aroma of the Shisha pipes, the locals sat in groups and smoked in the coffee shops. There were stalls of colourful spices displayed in perfect heaps. There were perfume shops, selling their perfume in beautifully blown glass bottles, the vendors encouraging the passers-by to buy their wares.

We decided to have Hussain as our regular driver, and would pay him at the end of each day, accordingly.

That night we dressed up in the traditional Egyptian dresses, we had purchased that afternoon and went out on the town, sampling the night life of the hustling and bustling streets of Cairo.

The following night, Hussain picked us up, to take us to Giza the site of the Pyramids, so we could sample the night life of the desert. We walked around taking in the glorious sights. Before Hussain was to take us back to the hotel, he wanted us to meet his friends, who lived not far from the Pyramids. We walked through some alleys to a small house belonging to his friend who had horses tied up in his yard. We admired the beautiful Arab horses. He asked us if we would like to have a ride on them. Well! An offer we could not refuse. The three of us had to pick a horse, and we took them for a ride in the desert. Since I was not confident at riding, I just rode away at a canter, the owner and Hussain guiding us on their horse back. It was getting quite late by the time we finished the ride. We had not had our dinner so we asked the boys if there was anywhere we could eat. They said that they could get us some snacks if we wished. So they rode back to some shops and brought back some snacks and beers.

It was the most beautiful experience, us sitting on the sand, having a midnight picnic, in the warmth of the desert, the sky full of twinkling stars, and the view of the Pyramids proudly standing in the distance.

Hussain promised to take us to Alexandria, which is the Mediterranean Port City, about 200 kilometres from Cairo. It took us just over three hours' drive to get there. We filled his car up with petrol for the journey. We had a couple of stops on the way at some fantastic restaurants.

Once we got there, we went up the harbour lighthouse where we had the beautiful view of the harbour and the city of Alexandria. We were driven back to our hotel by Hussain after a very tiring journey, just having one more stop on the way back, sailing on a felucca, on the River Nile.

The next day, we were taken to The Cairo Museum. As Hussain was driving through the streets, I noticed a hotel called "Cleopatra." This was the hotel we had stayed overnight at with our parents on the way to England, from Uganda. We didn't get too close to it, but it looked a bit run down, and didn't look at all flashy, as when we had stayed there.

At the Cairo Museum we saw all the Egyptian Antiques, the best of which was the finery of the boy King, Tutankhamun. His chariot, his beautiful furniture, his hunting tools, his golden jewellery, and best of all his golden funerary mask.

We were able to take a lot of videos and photos for our albums.

All these artefacts were discovered in 1925, by Howard Carter, who had discovered Tutankhamun's tomb in the Valley of the Kings.

We were very sad, when our holiday came to an end. We had had a very educational and fulfilling experience in Cairo.

Alan

It was back to work, I was moved to a different department, and was placed in Starburst, and later in Skittles.

Being a Temp, there was always a possibility of being moved to different departments, wherever the demand for workers was.

This was ideal, as we were able to learn new skills in each department.

I was busy packing away once, when a permanent member of staff approached me and asked me if I was married, or in a relationship. I asked him why he was interested to know that to which he replied that his mate had asked him to find out, what he could about me. I told him that I was single.

He must have conveyed the message to this person, who was asking about me, because later that day a man approached me and started chatting to me, while I was packing. He introduced himself as Alan. He made small talk, and seeing that I was busy soon left.

Then I started noticing him by the Clocking Machine, chatting to his friends, waiting for me to clock out, so he could chat to me. He gave me his phone number on a piece of paper, and said that it would be nice, if I could ring him sometimes.

I placed the paper in my bag. I did not ring him. I was not sure if I wanted to start seeing anyone anymore, after what I had gone through.

But Alan kept on insisting on taking me out for a drink.

Then one day I decided to take him up on his offer, and we made plans to meet in a pub.

We talked about each other, and I found that he was going through his divorce and was separated from his wife, and was staying with his dad at the time. He told me that he had a daughter and a son, of school-going age.

We would see each other at work and chat, whenever possible.

The Far East

My friends were planning another holiday, this time to countries in the Far East. I wasn't very sure, if I would be able to afford this holiday.

Tammy was not going to be able to go, as by now she had a baby girl. She had met a young Egyptian man in a club and had later got married to him. Cecilia too had met a young man called Robert and had got married to him, so she too wasn't able go. It was going to be Julia, Maria and her sister making plans to go. When I looked at the itinerary that Maria had prepared, I was so temped to join them. Julia offered to pay for part of my fare, which she said, I could pay back when we returned. I took her up on her offer. I told Alan that I was going on holiday with my friends, and would catch up with him on my return. Our journey began with a few nights in Hong Kong. We had an amazing time shopping in the Times Square and sampling the local food. We also did a lot of sightseeing, and had a boat trip in the South China Sea, where there were floating restaurants and boats selling vegetables, fruit and fish.

We took a flight to our second stop which was at Chiang Mai, in Thailand, where we stayed in a very colourful and traditional hotel. We went to see a few Buddhist Temples, and once again did some sightseeing.

The next stop was in Bangkok, an amazing city that was busy day and night. Once again we visited a few Buddhist temples and walked through the colourful markets. During the night time we would walk the streets that were busy with night clubs and food stalls. And sampled the delicious food.

We even tried a night club that was full of what we believed to be stunning girls, but turned out to be transvestites. One of them was singing a Tina Turner song, dressed in an outfit just like hers.

I was amazed to see young girls working on their scooters as taxis, and carrying passengers around. Though we didn't use them, as we would normally travel on Tuk- Tuk's.

Our last stop was to be on the Tropical Island of Koi Samui. Our hotel was on a beautiful beach. We had a lot of fun in the blue sea, and the hotel swimming pool. The food was out of this world.

I would use the stationery provided by each of the hotels we stayed at, to write a note to Alan, and post it. My friends were not aware of this as I didn't tell them about Alan. I wasn't even sure if he would want to know me after my holiday, as we had hardly got to know each other before I had set off.

In fact, I had had so many disappointments with men in my life in the past, I was planning to stay single. I had always hoped to find the right man and settle down, but failed to find a suitable match.

When I returned from our holiday, I wondered if Alan would still be interested in seeing me.

He welcomed me back and we started seeing each other. Soon I met his dad and his kids, his young daughter and his son. Our friendship soon turned into a relationship. He soon left his dad's place, which was meant to be temporary, while he was going through the process of a divorce with his wife, and started renting a bedsit. This made it easier for his kids to come and stay with him at weekends.

He took me on a holiday to Greece, which we enjoyed thoroughly.

Almost a year went by, and we went on yet another holiday to Greece, where Alan proposed to me, and I accepted his proposal.

Alan had a Yamaha Wild star 1600cc Motor bike, and sometimes he would give me a ride to work on it. We would also go on a leisurely ride on it.

A year after his bedsit contract was over, Alan moved in with me. I had run into some arrears with the rent, since I stopped getting any help towards it, due to Sirita leaving her school, and also the fact that as a Temp, I had stopped getting regular work at the factory. I would get a day or two each week, and I wasn't getting a sufficient wage at that time. Also having borrowed money for the holiday to Hong Kong and Thailand, from my friend did not help, as I had to pay that back too.

When Alan moved in with me, he was kind enough to clear my rent debts so we could start afresh.

We started making plans for our wedding. He wanted us to get married at the wedding chapel in Graceland, since he was a great fan of Elvis Presley. He was known for singing Elvis songs at Karaoke's, especially on holidays. He was very good at that.

We were planning our holiday in Las Vegas for our wedding at the Graceland chapel, but Sonal and Sirita wanted us to get married in England as they were in no position to afford to go to Las Vegas, and wanted to be present at our wedding.

So, we changed our plans and had a very small wedding on 20th September 2003, at the Maidenhead Registrar's office, with just a few of my friends, a couple of Alan's friends, his kids, his dad and his sister and her husband, and my daughters, Richard and Amie of course.

After having had one failed wedding, which my parents had spent hundreds of pounds on, I did not want any fuss on my second wedding.

My friend Tammy gave me a dress, she no longer needed, which I wore as my wedding dress. Maria too gave me a beautiful long dress that I wore in the evening. I did not fuss over having my hair done by a hairdresser or have my makeup done. I just washed it on the day and wore it like I always had and did my own makeup. I did not order any flowers apart from the wedding bouquet. I didn't need any fuss.

Due to the change of our wedding plans, we had to accept the earliest date we could get, at the Registrar's office. We were only planning for the very quiet wedding, but without my knowledge, my girls had invited more people than we had anticipated. They had invited my sister and her family too.

Our reception was held in our back garden, where we had erected a large gazebo.

One of my neighbourhood friends, Wendy, had arranged all the food, and had laid the table beautifully. She had also helped my daughters with the decorations, and balloons in the living room.

Even though it was the end of September, it happened to be a hot day, so we were very lucky to be able to have the reception in the garden.

That evening we left to stay at the Sheep House Manor, where I used to work, and had booked a night. We were given a chalet for the night, by my boss. She had left a complimentary bottle of champagne in an ice bucket for us, along with a breakfast tray for the morning.

A month after our wedding, we went on our honeymoon to Florida. We stayed in a Best Western Hotel, on the international drive.

We had purchased a pass for Disney World, so would take a mini bus to Disney Land, almost every day, and enjoy the rides and sights of Disney Land.

We had a great time, exploring Florida.

Alan's Family

Alan's dad had been very kind, and accepted me gladly as his daughter-in-law.

We would go to a pub and have a few drinks and chat. I would always buy him a whisky after he had had a few pints of beer, and he always appreciated it.

He loved listening to stories of my time in India and Africa. He would always ask me about my mum and praised me for seeing her regularly, and caring for her.

He loved going to the Irish Club and loved dancing. We accompanied him to the Irish club once, and he asked me to dance with him. I have never been able to dance, especially, the Jive.

But he took me in his arms and led me so elegantly to a waltz to the Irish folk music that I managed to dance with the flow.

We went on holiday with him a couple of times, once to Cornwall and then to a caravan park, and found him to be great company.

He had always been very sociable and made friends easily.

One would always find him chatting to any stranger he came across, no matter where he was.

Patrick had been a great support to Alan, when he was going through his separation and divorce. Alan had moved in with his dad, till he sorted himself out. The pair would have a good drinking session in the evening, watching their favoured DVD's, watching football, or just talking about this, that and everything, this helped them form a great father and son relationship.

Alan's family had come from Kerry, in Ireland, where most of Patrick's and his late mum's siblings still lived.

His sister and her husband too had a holiday home in Kerry, in Ireland, though they were settled in England with their three children, a boy and two girls, and the house in Kerry was used as a holiday house.

Our Move to Cippenham

Soon after Alan and I had got married, Sirita started looking for a place to rent. Not long after, she found herself a flat in Cippenham, in Slough. She moved all her belongings in there, with the help of her friends, and settled in well. She asked my brother, Gulab, to help her with the deposit, which he kindly agreed. Unfortunately, she was a bit slow paying it back, for she had all the bills to pay, and had hardly any money left over at the end of the month.

She found herself an evening job at a local pub, serving behind the bar. This helped her pay off her debts.

I felt sorry for her, yet was very proud of her, for standing on her own two feet.

We soon planned to move house, as the area we lived in started getting a bit rough. The neighbourhood cars were either being damaged by youths or stolen.

We managed to get a transfer into a property in Cippenham, in Slough through the housing association and settled into our new home. The new property was closer to our work in Mars, so that was handy for us.

As Alan and I were on the same shift pattern, we would travel to and from work together.

A new department manufacturing Twixels was launched, and Alan was placed into the Processing department, in charge of making caramel. Most of the processing was done by

Robotic machines, but the packing had to be done manually. I was transferred into this department, so Alan and I were working close by.

Whenever the production lines were shutdown, it was time for maintenance and cleaning. The cleaning would mostly be done by the Temps. We would have to clean the huge ovens that cooked the biscuits. We would have to scrape all the walls of the ovens, of its dried up biscuit dough and then hoover the whole oven up, and clean with rolls of anti-bac till it was all spotless. It was dark in the ovens, apart from the natural light, so we would have to use a torch to guide us with the cleaning. At the end of our cleaning, the manager would inspect each corner of the oven, in order to make sure that we had done a good job.

I was encouraged by my Temping manager to learn to drive an electric pallet truck.

I had some training and managed to pass my test. So now I was able to help with transferring and moving pallets, which had cases of finished product, from the department to either the warehouse or the collection point.

Another job would be to take the full skips, which either contained raw material for reprocessing or rubbish, to the skip yard.

There was a funny incident, once when I was taking the skip, for the skip yard. It had to be transported by a lift, as our department was on the first floor.

As I pressed the button for the ground floor, the lift started moving then stopped midway. It was jammed and I couldn't get it going, so I pressed the emergency button. The factory emergency siren started blaring, and soon I heard voices outside the lift.

I would have been visible from my legs to my waist, to the emergency team. The engineer managed to fix the problem within minutes, and the lift moved back to the top. And to my surprise, Alan, along with our manager and a few other emergency team members were stood outside, to make sure that I was okay. I was quite embarrassed when the lift doors opened, to see them all standing there.

Alan had done his fire safety and First aid course and was in the emergency team. When the alarm was set, it would be announced on the Tannoy, to where the emergency was, and the emergency team members, nearest to the emergency, would drop whatever they would be doing and rush to the emergency.

I would always talk to Alan about the great holidays I had had in Egypt, and would encourage him to try it too. He decided to give it a go.

We booked a Nile Cruise, and flew over to Luxor for our holiday.

As we boarded the boat and were shown to our cabin, Alan was not too sure if he was going to like this kind of a holiday.

He soon started enjoying the experience, when all the activities and the sightseeing tours started.

We did all the stops on this cruise to the various sites and temples, as I had done on my previous Nile Cruise.

We made so many friends on the boat, as we would all take part in the tours and activities. We had a great group of people on board.

We also managed to fly on a hot air balloon, like I had done previously.

We ended up having the greatest night on the last night of the cruise, with fancy dress and dancing.

Alan and I dressed up in the Egyptian outfits.

After this holiday, we went on yet another Nile Cruise. We also went to Cairo and had a few holidays in Luxor.

By this time Alan too had fallen in love with Egypt.

Whilst on holiday in Cairo, we did a lot of sightseeing and went to the Cairo museum, which I had already done with my friends previously. And also went to visit the pyramids.

Towards the end of this marvellous holiday I suddenly felt a burning sensation on the left side of my face. I couldn't eat properly and felt like I was dribbling. I had a burning sensation in my mouth as well, and found that the food didn't taste like it used to. There would be a sharp pain on my left cheek starting from my mouth to my head. I would repel, if anyone came close to the left side of my face. My lips felt like, they were made of rubber, and tingled all the time.

Upon our return, I went to see my doctor and was sent to Wexham Park Hospital, to the Neurological Department.

A load of tests was carried on, yet they couldn't find the cause or cure for my problem. During the cold season my face would go numb and cold. The feeling I would have was like I had Bell's palsy, but was told that this wasn't the case.

I was then referred to the Neurology department at the University College Hospital London, for investigation.

I went through various tests and had to stay over on several occasions, as an in-patient for them to investigate my problem.

I had MRI scans and CT scans done. I also had a Lumber Puncture done, and at last came up with a name for my condition, which was Holmes Adie Syndrome. This is described as a viral or bacterial infection, which causes inflammation and damage to the autonomic nervous system, and causes abnormally dilated pupil in one eye and reacts slowly to light, thus makes strong light unbearable.

It also causes the patient a chronic cough. There is loss of deep tendon abnormalities of sweating, where one side of the body can stay dry, and the other half sweat profusely during a hot day, and during a workout.

For this, I had a couple of Thermal Threshold tests done, which proved that the affected left side of my body did not sweat, yet the right side would sweat more than usual, and I had to regularly go to the appointments, for more tests.

Even though I had various tests, I was never offered any kind of treatment.

New addition to our family

On the 4th of September 2005. My second grand daughter was born. Richard and Sonal decided to call her Nicola, but when she arrived, Sonal thought that she should be named Holly. So, she was named Holly Nicola Townsend. She was a beautiful baby, just like Amie had been. I was very proud to be a Nani to such beautiful granddaughters.

As Holly was growing up, I had loads of opportunities to baby sit her. She was a very pleasant child to look after.

When I took her shopping, she would never demand any treats, like sweets and crisps or toys, and would be happy with whatever I bought for her.

Sonal had always disciplined her daughters and they were brought up not to be demanding.

Sonal returned to work after she had served her maternity term, so Holly had to be looked after by a friend of Sonal's. I would try and have her whenever I could.

Whenever I visited Sonal, Holly would want me to play with her, with her toys. Her favourite playtime was playing shopkeepers, with her toy shop, with mini groceries and plastic fruit and vegetables. She loved playing the shopkeeper as she got the chance of working her toy till machine with paper money, and I often ended up being her customer.

When Holly started her Primary schooling, she would stay behind for her after school class, to be picked up by Sonal, after finishing work.

This arrangement suited both Holly and Sonal.

Sonal and Richard managed to juggle work and looking after their girls very well.

Our Holiday home in Sharm-el-Sheikh

After our last holiday to Egypt, Alan got talking to our manager about the lovely holiday we had had. The manager told him that he too loved Egypt. Along with his wife, who was also a manager at the Mars Factory, he decided to take their redundancy, and move to Sharm-el-Sheikh and work as diving instructors.

He showed him the property he had purchased, and said that there were more properties going up for sale, in the same complex.

This is when Alan got tempted, and ended up buying a one-bedroom apartment in Sharm-el-Sheikh.

It was still in its construction stage, when he purchased it.

When our manager moved to his newly built apartment in Sharm-el-Sheikh, he started sending us photos of the stages of building work in order to update us.

We couldn't wait for it to be completed, eager to start using it, as our holiday home.

In the year 2006, we flew to Sharm-el-Sheikh to our new holiday home.

We were picked up in a taxi and taken to the "Egyptian Experience Complex" in Nabq Bay

where we were greeted by the manager, who after all the formalities took us to our apartment.

It was a fully furnished ground floor apartment, consisting of a bedroom, a wet room and a furnished kitchen with a sitting area. Through the patio door was a patio, with a table and chairs, and some steps leading to a shared swimming pool, which was literally at our doorstep.

We were so elated to call this beautiful apartment our own.

At the main entrance stood all the two, and three-bedroom luxury apartments, with a main pool we went for a walkabout around the complex, in order to get familiarised with the place.

Right in the middle of them. In fact, all the blocks of apartments had their own swimming pool. Ours happened to be the second biggest.

When on top of the terrace roof, we could see the Sharm-el-Sheikh airport. In fact, part of its border met up with our complex, dividing it with just a wire fence. Also visible were the Sinai Mountains from the roof top. We would often witness a beautiful sunset, the sun disappearing behind the Sanai Mountains, making the sky go golden, yellow and red colours.

All the planes from the airport would fly over our heads, when taking off.

On the other side was the main road which, if crossed, would take us to the Red Sea. Naama Bay was the main tourist beach with stunning views of the Gulf of Aqaba, where people went to swim, scuba -dive amongst the corals and also go snorkelling. This was the city, with all the shops and banks, along with luxury hotels, and bars run by people from Russia and Britain. The British had given their bars British names, like The Three Crowns, Union Jack, Jive Bar, Bus stop, etc.

There was a lot of construction work taking place all around, with new hotels and shops being built with the upcoming of this newly built city. Some of the Egyptians had given their shops English names like Totty Market, George Clooney. There was also a shop called Asda, which sold souvenirs and gifts.

Most of the residents of this complex were the British who, either moved here to settle down, or used it as a holiday home, like we did.

We started visiting our apartment every year, though Alan would visit it at least twice, as he would take either his daughter or his son, on holiday with him.

We had Sirita accompany us, a couple of times too. We went on a ride on Quad Bikes, in the Sinai Desert sands, and also did some horse riding in the Sinai Desert on beautiful Arab horses. We started our ride with a large group of riders, at late afternoon and headed back at dusk. On our way back from the ride, unfortunately Sirita was thrown off her horse, when some Quad Bikes roared past us, and her horse panicked and bolted in fear. She was left standing there in the dark desert, where the only light was from the moon light and the stars. Her horse just ran off towards the stables where we had started our ride from. Luckily my horse had been led by the stable boy, by its lead, as I was not an experienced rider. He came to Sirita's aid, flashing his torch in her direction, making sure that she was okay. He rang the stables for assistance, and soon a jeep arrived. I let Sirita ride my horse back to the stables, and I took a ride back in the jeep.

This had been an amazing experience for us though a bit scary too, as the Bedouin tribe lived in the Sinai desert, and they were known to loot tourists. How true this was, I'm not sure.

We started going to our apartment regularly.

Just as well we had had travelled to various places, before purchasing the apartment, like Sri Lanka, Dubai, a few trips to Malta, and to Tenerife and at least three trips to Maspalomas, which are the Canary Islands - all of which were fantastic holidays and experiences.

Moving back to Dundee Road

A year into working in the Twixels Department, the whole of the factory plant at the Liverpool road was to be shut down, and moved to Europe. All the workers, the permanent and the temporary staff had to be moved into the sister plant at Dundee Road.

Some of the permanent staff took an early retirement or redundancy.

The Temps were placed wherever the need was.

I was lucky to be able to get regular work, provided I was happy to work in any department.

Alan moved into the Dundee Road factory, but didn't settle in there for long. He too decided to go for his redundancy, as he was going to get a generous package by doing so.

He went back to his plastering, which he had done since he left school. He had achieved the Guilds Certificate, and has been a master at plastering.

The number of times, he has pointed out to me that he had plastered certain places, as we drove by them, is uncountable.

He decided to go self-employed, and worked for various builders.

Since he left the Mars factory, it was not ideal for me to work twelve hours shifts, especially the night shifts, so I asked my manager to put me on day shifts only.

This was a hard decision to make, as my hours would be cut down, as well as losing my Team Leader's job.

I was offered a job, doing the payroll in the office for the Temps. I was given some guidance by my manager, and started the job. I worked from 7am to 3pm on Mondays only, as that was the day we did the payroll for the week. I was slow at picking up the skills, but my manager was very patient with me, and helped me whenever I got stuck. It was strange going into work, in normal clothes, instead of the factory whites.

I started buying some smart clothes, suitable for the office job.

I would feel awkward going into the canteen and be seen by my colleagues.

I would be on stand-by the rest of the week and would try to get a few day shifts in the factory.

I had the opportunity to work in R & D as well, where new products were created, though I was more of a helping hand than a creator.

At one such time, when I had been doing a shift in the factory, I was sat in the canteen having a lunch break, when one of our Temps joined me, and while chatting, he mentioned about the new girl who had started working in payroll, in the office.

I had to tell him that, this new girl happened to be me. He just couldn't believe me.

I had always been seen wearing my whites, with heavy steel toes, black boots, with my hair in a net and a hard hat. I must have looked like a different person in my smart clothes.

Few months into my office job, Alan and I ended up going to our apartment in Egypt, for at least three weeks. On our return, I found that my job had been given to another Temp.

Now I was back on the factory floor, working from one department to another.

I was once given a job of transporting ready stacked pallets from various departments to the warehouse. This left the Temps on the line to carry on packing and stacking, instead of wasting time on transporting the finished pallets to the warehouse.

I even mastered working the double pallet truck, so I could take twice the amount on each journey.

When there were quiet moments, I would be asked to clean and sweep around the warehouse floors, where the sweets had fallen out of broken packaging.

I enjoyed doing this job, as it made me feel independent, and I would take my tea or lunchbreak whenever I wished. There were some disadvantages in not having a permanent shift, because when the lines were shut down due to maintenance, the likes of me were the last on the list of priority for a job, and I would go without a job for days. Work for the Temps was scarce, because the permanent staff that had been moved from the Liverpool Road Factory were given the first priority. Some of the Temps had to leave, from lack of work. I was getting just a couple of days' work each week.

I too ended up falling into this category, after ten years of working in the Mars Confectionery Factory, so unfortunately had to give in my notice.

Arun

Since my divorce with Arun, surprisingly I had never bumped into him or had any contact with him, which I was glad about. I would hear of his welfare through my mum, who would have heard of it through Didi and my brother-in-law.

Before Didi's passing, he had been seeing them, and had apparently made up. I had also heard through my mum that he had re-married and that his health was not good.

Then I heard that he had passed away.

I never ever wanted to see him but had never wished him pain or sorrow.

I did not attend his funeral.

I told Sonal and Sirita, of the bad news, and asked them if they wanted to go to a Hindu temple to pay their respects with a prayer.

They were happy to do that, so we made some offerings at the temple and said a prayer for him.

Self Employed

I started searching for work elsewhere, but jobs were hard to come by.

In my desperation, I decided to go for a cleaning job, perhaps in a hotel or at the Airport, but was unsuccessful with every application I made.

Then I saw an advert in the local paper, where a lady was looking for cleaners. I got in touch with her and fortunately she was happy to take me on.

I would either share a job with her or go on a job on my own, till she found another young girl to join the team, and then she would team us both up.

The pay for this cleaning job was not as good as what I earned at the Factory, but I was pleased that I had at least found a job, hoping that I would keep searching for another suitable job soon.

I was getting a lot of appointments from the UCLH hospital for my condition, when I would have to take time off. My lady boss did not take kindly to me taking time off. Even when I wanted to go on our annual holiday, she would create a fuss.

I understood that she did not have sufficient staff to cover my absence, but also felt that I was being put under pressure for taking time off.

After a couple of years working for her, I decided to go solo and build up my own business where I could earn more money and have the flexibility of attending my hospital appointments, visiting my mum and taking my holidays, without any hassle.

My friend Maria's sister mentioned that she knew a few people who were looking for a cleaner. When I went to meet with them, they were happy to give me a job.

So, I gave in my notice to my boss, and set up my little cleaning business. Through word of mouth and my few existing customers, my clientele increased.

Since I left the job with my boss, she struggled to fulfill the needs of her existing customers, and ended up terminating her contract with them.

I felt very guilty about leaving her, but then it was her business, and she could easily have found more staff.

Being self-employed now, I appointed the same accountant as Alan.

My business grew, and I was doing at least two to three jobs a day, and earning a reasonable wage.

A couple of the families, who had their contract terminated by my ex-boss were desperately in need of a cleaner, and asked me if I could clean for them. Since I had already worked for them previously, I was happy to take the jobs.

Andy was one such customer, who had three kids - two boys and a girl. One of the boys and the daughter were primary school age and the youngest went to a nursery.

Andy would ask me to clean the little boy's room first, as he always had a nap after nursery.

Andy's kids were growing fast, and they soon had an addition to their family, a puppy named Bentley, a Field Cocker Spaniel.

He was so beautiful with his chocolate coloured shiny fur.

He was the gentlest dog I had ever come across and was especially very good with children.

I had never been a fan of animals, as I happened to be allergic to animal fur and was always scared when cats and dogs came close to me, but Bentley was such an obedient and calm dog, that I never feared him.

All my customers were very kind and friendly towards me. There were families having new born babies, and I witnessed them growing up, during the time I cleaned for them.

Primary school kids going into secondary schools, and secondary school kids starting college.

As I cleaned the children's rooms for the families with kids, I would come across the latest toys and trends, on the floor or their desks to be tidied up.

In the year 2010, the trend was of the Rainbow loom rubber bands. It was mainly young girls, who would create beautiful bracelets, or keychains out of colourful rubber bands. I would come across these rubber bands all over the carpets, which were very hard to hoover up.

The boys would have their Marvel toy figurines all over their bedrooms. They would also have the air guns with Nerf toy soft bullets. I would find the soft bullets all over the house.

Then came the trend of the Fidget finger Spinners in 2017. The kids had multi- coloured, and various designs of spinners.

Not forgetting the Lego bricks. There would be Castles, and Star wars, Lego sets, fancy cars and cranes and all sorts created by the kids. I would be worried that I might dismantle their creation by touching them, and was very conscious whilst cleaning around them. I did in fact have a few accidents, but luckily, with only a few pieces coming loose.

Kitties

Since Sirita had been little, she had always wanted a pet. She was very fond of animals, whereas Sonal and I were not very keen.

I had got her a rabbit, when I lived in our house in Maidenhead, which had to stay in the garden. Soon she was given another rabbit. They bred, like rabbits do, and we ended up with a few rabbits hopping about in our garden. They destroyed most of my lawn and plants, and the mother rabbit would kick me, whenever I went to hang my washing on the line.

I was actually scared of her.

Soon, it all got out of control, and I was forced to take all the rabbits to the Animal sanctuary.

Sirita cried her eyes out as she gave her pet rabbits the last hug.

After a while she got a gerbil. It was only allowed in her bedroom. So, she would place it in a ball and let it roll around the house.

Luckily that was the last pet she had.

But then in 2015, when she lived in her own flat, she decided to get herself a cat.

I accompanied her to look for one at various Battersea Homes, just to get an idea of what she really wanted.

Then, one day we had Holly with us and we decided to go again. Both Sirita and Holly fell in love with a little ginger kitten that was so playful and was doing high-fives with us. It would hide in its cat tree, then pop out again, like it was playing peekaboo with us. We thought that it was so cheeky.

When we enquired about it, we were told that it was a male kitten, of a litter of three. Sirita knew that he was the right one for her. She offered to get him when he was at the right age to leave its mummy. Then out of the cat-tree appeared another little black and white kitten. We played with it too, and were told that it was a female. By now Sirita wanted both the kittens.

She ended up with both, and named cheeky kitten Charlie and his sister was named Lola.

Charlie and Lola have been great cats, they are ever so friendly with strangers, and have been house trained since Sirita got them. They are a great company for Sirita too.

Losing Patrick

In the year 2016 we got some sad news that Alan's dad had contracted cancer due to asbestosis. He had worked in construction, working with pre- cast concrete, which was used for the building of M4, and later, on the building of M25. Some of the material used in the manufacturing of such concrete contained asbestos. He had been in this industry since he came to England from Ireland, in search of work.

Alan took some time off work, so he could spend more time with his dad. He would visit him daily and kept him company, and at last when his dad started deteriorating, he helped him towards his hygiene needs.

Alan's sister's husband built a wet room downstairs of Patrick's house so he could have a shower and access to the toilet, and not have to climb the stairs to go upstairs.

His sister and the grandchildren too visited him regularly, and would take him out for meals. Everyone in the family tried to make his life as comfortable as they could.

Soon after that, as Patrick's condition worsened, the Macmillan nurses would come and take care of him.

Sadly, he passed away in December 2016.

He is missed by all the family.

Our New Home

In the year 2017 Alan decided that we moved, and bought our own property.

He was keen on moving into a park home, for that was the only way he could afford a reasonable property. We looked at a few homes in the park home in Windsor, but I was not keen on them, as they were very small.

One of his friends got talking to him and said that his Mother had passed away, and was trying to sell her park home, at the same site as we had looked before.

We went to view the property, and I soon fell in love with it.

It had three bedrooms, the main one with an ensuite, a bathroom, a large sitting room, with a dining area.

The gardens around the property were vast.

We soon signed the contract with his friend and moved into the new property which is situated by, and has access to, the River Thames.

Alan's dad's inheritance helped a lot towards the buying of the property.

Over the years in this property, we spent a lot of money to better the garden and the bathroom and the shower room.

We found this place very peaceful and comfortable, as most of the people living here happened to be elderly, and a friendly lot.

We often walked to the Windsor Town centre, which was nice to do, when there was some sort of ceremony going on at the Windsor Castle.

The walk to the Thames River was literally minutes, and it was nice to sit by the river and see the swans and the boats go by.

My Mum

I started visiting my mum a lot, as she always had doctor's appointments to keep. It had fallen upon my aunty to take her to her appointments, for when she visited my mum, she would persuade her to arrange an appointment for her, and then take her to her appointments. Soon there were hospital appointments to attend, and I found that it was not fair on her to be given the task of the well-being of our mum.

Our mum had always been independent in her 70s and 80s. She would catch a bus to go to her local supermarket, and was regularly visiting my aunty. She was able to travel around, using her Bus Pass. She would sometimes change two buses to get her to Slough to visit my brother-in-law, his new wife and the grandchildren.

But during her late 80s she kind of became a recluse. She had rather people came to visit her, and she did not want to leave her flat.

She would only go out, if she was picked up by a member of the family.

This all started when once she had gone down to answer the front door and found a couple of young lads at her doorstep. She could not understand what they were talking about, so went to shut the door, but then one of the lads pushed her against the wall and started pulling her gold bangles off her wrist. They were very tight on her wrist, so he was unable to take them off. My mum struggled to get away from him and started screaming and shouting. The lads panicked when they saw a neighbour with his dog passing by. Then one of them just grabbed her gold chain off her neck and fled leaving her in shock.

This incident made her very nervous to go out of the flat.

She did not want to answer the door to anyone after her ordeal. We had keys cut, one for each of our family and one for our aunty, so that we could let ourselves in, when visiting her, and we made sure that we phoned her in advance to let her know that we were visiting her.

My mum had had some stents put in to her arteries due to having angina. She was also diabetic, and suffered from high blood pressure. So, she was always under constant observation by the doctors.

She made her regular visits to the West Middlesex hospital, for her check-ups along with her eye tests, due to her diabetes, so it was essential that someone took her to her appointments. My brother, Gulab, was always at hand, if I was unable to take her.

My mum kept an address book, with all the families' and friends' addresses and phone numbers. She had jotted, on top of each address, the name of the person, in Hindi, as a guide, so as to know whose address it was, when posting birthday and Christmas cards. My brother Ashok's son and daughter used to buy notebooks for my mum, when she had moved to Peterborough, and make her practise writing the English alphabet, and writing sentences from a book, so she was quite good at copying the addresses on the envelopes.

She had also written notes of how to write Happy Birthday, or Happy Christmas, and would follow these notes when sending cards.

She also had a diary, with the family members' birth dates, so she would refer to it each week, so that she would not forget to send us cards.

She was not a big spender when it came to buying things for herself, but loved giving us all money, on occasions such as Christmas and birthdays.

Gulab had set up several saving plans for her, like Shares and ISA's when she had lived with him in Swindon. She was receiving her old age pension, my dad's Air Canada pension as well as his Uganda pension.

Her flat had all been paid for, which Gulab, Ashok and my mum had jointly purchased. So, she only had her utility and food bills to pay for. Her old age pension usually covered these.

She would always put money in the cards she sent us. She would rather do that, than get us gifts that often didn't get used.

We always discouraged her to place cash in the cards in case it got lost in the post.

So, she started sending us cheques. At times she would make a mistake writing the cheque, so I decided to write the cheques on her behalf and let her sign them, before posting them

This became a bit laborious during Christmas times, as she would end up sending cheques to all the family members. I would write out the cards, then the addresses and the cheques that took her ages to sign.

Rakish would volunteer to do them every now and then, in order to give me a break.

There were times when her chequebook would run out and she had to order a new one, in time for Christmas.

It felt awkward when I had to write a card and cheque to myself on her behalf.

When I took her for her grocery shopping she would pay by cash, till the time she got her bank card with a PIN number. She would place her card in a little purse along with the PIN number jotted on a piece of paper.

When at the till, in time for paying, she would insert her card into the card reader and then read out her PIN number loud enough for everyone to hear. I would ask her to be very careful, for there were always fraudsters lurking around. I also worried that she might lose her purse, with her card and the PIN number easily available to the finder.

Upon visiting her regularly, I started noticing that she was getting forgetful. She would tell me that no one had visited her, whereas I knew that my brothers, my brother-in-law and his wife, my aunty or my sister had paid her a visit regularly.

First of all, we put her behaviour down to her seeking attention.

She would complain that no one bothered to visit her anymore, and that she was very lonely. Over the years she got worse. She was not having regular baths, or changing herself, her hair would be unkempt. She was forgetting how to change the channels on her television along with stopping her ritual of saying her prayers in the morning, which she had done every morning after a shower, and before having breakfast. She had done this as far back as I can remember.

I used to take my granddaughter, Holly, over to her on the days I looked after her. We would let ourselves in, and as we went up to her living room, I would find her in her bedroom saying her prayers, in front of the make shift Mandir, (Temple) she had created, with framed pictures of all the Indian gods and little statues of the idols. We would smell the scent of the incense she was burning, along with a little purpose built lamp burning using ghee and a rolled up cotton wool as its wick, known as a diva, a small tray with offerings and fruit, surrounded by fresh flowers.

She would not even acknowledge us till she had finished her prayers, and sung a few religious hymns.

I would get irritated with her for not acknowledging us, and taking her time with her prayers.

But now, with her deteriorating condition, I wished that she was back to how she was then, and that I would put up with her delay in acknowledging us, and not be impatient with her.

She had always been set in her ways, there was a set time for every day chores.

She would wash her hair on Mondays, and do her washing on Mondays as well, then Tuesday she would do her ironing. Everything had to be ironed, including the towels and tea towels.

She always wore salwar kameez, a traditional Indian dress, even when she went to bed.

She used to always dress up in a sari, when we lived in Uganda, but since she started working at Trust House Forte, she wore salwar kameez for safety reasons, and thus got used to wearing them. The beautiful saris were only worn when she went to visit people or at parties.

I remember buying her a couple of bottles of washing liquid, which happened to be white in colour, and left them on the kitchen worktop. The next time I visited her, I found these bottles, placed in her fridge. She had mistaken them for milk. I was glad to find that she had not yet used them, and had to place them under the sink unit.

She had always been addicted to watching Bollywood movies. But now if I was watching one with her, she would ask me what they were talking about, and I had to explain to her.

Quite often she would end up pressing buttons on her Sky remote control, and then panic if she couldn't watch her movies. She would ring me or the other members of the family, to go and sort her TV out, which was not always convenient, so she would have to go without any form of entertainment till one of us could get to her.

I discussed her condition with my brothers and my sister and we all decided to have her assessed by her doctor. Upon doing the appropriate tests on her, the doctors confirmed that she was in her early stages of dementia.

She was to soon start attending the Memory Clinic, where they would assess her condition every six months. The doctors tried putting her on various medications, to slow down her dementia, but unfortunately they did not suit her, so she had to give up on them.

She would be in perfect form some days, and yet, some days she would not be herself.

My brothers Gulab and Ashok made arrangements to celebrate our mum's 90th Birthday in style, which fell in May 2016. All of us siblings got together, and my aunty and had a great dinner party in a posh hotel. At that age she was still mobile and able to interact with us all.

Still slowly but surely, her condition got worse.

I once walked into her living room, after letting myself in her flat, and found her holding one of her photos in her hand. It was taken on her 60th birthday, where she looked so young. As she saw me, she asked me if the person in the photo was her. When I replied that it was, she kept on staring at it, I guess, thinking how young she was, once.

Though, despite being in her nineties, our mum had no sign of wrinkles. She always looked younger than her age.

We all started visiting her often to make sure that she was okay.

We would take some food for her, so that she wouldn't have to cook, but sometimes, the food would still be in the fridge untouched.

We would leave fresh fruit for her, to last her a few days, but at times that too would be still sitting in her fruit bowl.

I decided to visit her twice a week, and the rest of the week, the other members of our family would visit her in order to make sure that she had eaten.

My brother-in-law, his wife, along with my niece would visit my mum almost every weekend taking her favourite food for her.

The worse thing was that she would forget to take her medication.

Then we requested the doctor to introduce a blister pack for her medication. This still didn't work, as we would find that she still forgot to take it.

She was appointed an occupational therapist, who would regularly visit her.

She was provided with a fob, which she could press in an emergency; she hardly used it for the purpose it was for, but had numerous accidental calls to the emergency services.

She would accidently press it, while she was sleeping, and an ambulance would turn up at her door.

On their arrival, they would end up ringing me or Gulab, as we had provided them with our telephone numbers in case of emergency. As my mum couldn't communicate with them in English, one of us would have to go over to the flat to make sure that all was well. There had been numerous false alarms in a very short time, so we decided to take her fob off, as we felt that we were wasting the emergency ambulance's time.

Since she lived in a sheltered accommodation the panic alarm had already been installed in her house with the red cords to pull, in all her rooms, in case of an emergency.

Despite all the help we were giving her, it was not enough, and her condition was deteriorating. She had also become incontinent.

She would not drink enough water, so was always dehydrated, and would end up suffering from UTI. This made her irritable and moody.

Due to her cognitive impairment, our family appointed Gulab to take care of all her finances and along with Ashok, to have the power of attorney.

We soon decided that all the siblings get together and discuss her condition, and the help we could provide for her, in order to make her as comfortable as possible. We had numerous meetings, meeting up in a hired property in various parts of the country. This gave us an opportunity to have a mini holiday break, and be able to discuss our mum's welfare.

These meetings brought all of us very close as a family as generally, we were all busy in our jobs, and hardly saw each other. The fact that we all lived far from each other did not help.

We would occasionally get together at my mum's flat.

Seeing us all together made her very happy, and the fact that we would all eat together, and this encouraged her to eat more than she usually did.

But yet, she would be very sad when we all said our goodbyes and left her on her own again.

My brother Gulab took upon himself into looking for a home carer for her and soon had a carer appointed, who would come in the mornings to give her a shower, then her breakfast and medication.

The carer would update us regularly, with a phone call.

She was a great lady, who was kind and gentle with our mum. She was the only person, apart from Rakish, who was able to persuade our mum to have a shower. Since the carer was appointed, whenever I visited my mum in the afternoons for my regular visit, she would appear well groomed, with her hair in a neat plait, and dressed in clean clothes. This showed and gave us the satisfaction that the carer was doing a great job.

We ended up taking necessary steps to make things easy for our mum and ourselves.

I decided to replace the cord that held her salwars which had to be knotted to hold it in place, with elastic, so that it would be easier for her to just slip her salwar down, when she visited the toilet, for she had been having accidents, due to taking time to unknot the cord.

Soon we had to introduce her to Tena Pants.

Since mum lived on the first floor of the flat, we had a key safe installed, so that the carer or any official visiting her could let themselves into the flat, if the family members were not present.

Luckily, there had already been a stair lift installed in the flat by the previous owner. We would use this often, when my mum had to be taken anywhere. It also came in handy for the ambulance service paramedics, whenever they needed to transport our mum from the first floor to the ambulance.

The National Health Officer was appointed, to access our mum's mobility. The NHS ended up installing rails in her bathroom and her bedroom, to hold on to for safety. They also installed safety rails on her bed so that she did not fall out of her bed.

We started a diary, where whoever visited her would jot a note in it, documenting her condition, and what she had eaten that day, and the time they had spent with her. This gave us an indication of her day to day life.

The Care Company too had a register, which they had to fill in upon each visit. Both these logs helped the family be aware of the welfare of our mum.

We would still leave food for her, to be had for her lunch or dinner, but was again not eaten.

Then, Gulab found a lady who would come over at lunch time, heat up the food we had left in the fridge and make sure that my mum had a hot meal and a hot cup of tea. This was very reassuring for us. She, too, would keep a log of what our mum had eaten on daily basis.

As the time went on, we had to appoint an evening carer as well, to make sure that my mum's Tena Pants had been changed, because she might not have changed them herself since the morning change. And also, that she had had a hot drink, with her night time medication, before bed. The night time carer would change her into her bed clothes, and put her to bed, before leaving.

Mum had had a fall once while getting out of her bed. The morning carer had found her on the floor unable to pick herself up. She ended up hurting her arm, which resulted in her finding it very difficult to raise her left arm.

This also made dressing her very difficult, as she would scream, when we tried putting her kameez on her.

The only solution was to get her some pyjamas, with front fastening buttons.

This did the trick, and she not only found it painless, whilst being dressed, but also she looked so cute in them too.

All her salwar kameezes ended up in her wardrobe, never to be used again.

My job gave me the flexibility to visit her Monday and Friday afternoons, so these two days, the evening carer and the lunch time lady did not have to attend, as I fed her and put her to bed after going through her hygiene routine. At this point, my siblings decided that they should pay me for the time I gave my mum. Their idea for paying me was, because of my cleaning job. I could have found a job, during the hours I was spending with my mum, and the fact that I took her to most of her hospital appointments. I would have happily done this without being paid but my siblings kindly insisted, and Gulab arranged a payment made to me from our mum's funds.

Every evening, before I left my mum, I would make sure that she had had a hot drink, and give her tablets. After tucking her in bed, I would massage her legs, which gave her comfort. She kind of knew, that after the massage, I would be saying good-bye to her, so she would let me carry on to keep me there a bit longer.

I always felt very guilty, for every time I was about to leave her for the night, she would ask me to stay over and keep her company, for she felt lonely when she was left alone, but I always left her, reassuring her that I would be back soon. It would kill me, hearing her say in a soft voice, "Nobody stays with me! Nobody loves me!"

I would drive home, tears pouring down, warm against my cheeks, having the feeling of a mother leaving her helpless young child behind, alone, promising them that they would be back soon.

During the winter times, we would leave a hot water bottle under her covers, before putting her into bed, in order that she was warm. Despite her storage heating being on, she always felt cold, and wrapped herself in her duvet.

The morning carer would empty the bottle and put it away.

One afternoon when I went to visit her, she complained that a certain man had come to her flat and taken the baby away from her. I could not work out who this man could have been, and of course there was no baby in the flat. I also wondered if my brother-in-law had been to see her with his granddaughter, and that it was her she was talking about. So I put her behaviour down to perhaps a dream she might have had, because this conversation was repeated several times over the weeks.

Then one evening when I placed the hot water bottle in her bed, and put her to bed, she started cuddling the bottle, and saying that she was pleased that her baby was back. She would speak in a tone, one would use to talk like a baby. She would tell the baby never to leave her alone, like everyone else did.

This made me realise that she got comfort out of the bottle, and that her brain had taken her to her childhood. I often heard her talking in such a tone to the bottle, when I put her to bed, and was getting ready to leave.

The hot water bottle became a great part of her life.

Rakish found her a hot water bottle, its cover made like a doll's dress. We started placing the new bottle in her bed, which gave comfort to her.

My mum would spend most of her day in bed, and if the carer left her on her sofa, she would be found fast asleep on the sofa, if any one of us visited her. There were times when the family members visited her, she would not want to leave her bed. So, upon my brother Gulab's daughter Sharon's advice, we ordered a hospital bed for her, from the National Health to place in her living room, so she would spend her day and night in the living room.

She had also been provided with a wheel chair, and few other aids for her safety and comfort.

Every time Rakish would visit her, she would drive my mum to a local park in Osterley, and then put her in the wheel chair and walk along the lake, where our mum would benefit from the fresh air, some sun and a change of scenery to her daily routine. She took pleasure in feeding the ducks and swans.

The day time carers, as well as the night time carers were a godsend, along with the lunch time lady, for they kept us updated with my mum's condition, and we felt satisfied that someone was with our mum at least three times a day.

If for some reason my mum's condition was bad, they would call an ambulance out for her, and give one of our family members time to get to her in hospital, if need be.

We found that the food we used to leave in the fridge had not been eaten. The lunch time lady told us that she could only manage to feed my mum, a few spoonfuls of food.

Rakish bought tiny little plastic tubs, the ones used for storing baby's food, for us to store food in, as that's all she could manage to eat now.

Our mum's health was deteriorating fast, and yet looking at her features, at the ripe age of over ninety, she displayed no wrinkles on her face.

Though my mum had dementia, she still remembered our names and recognised us when we saw her. She could tell who she was talking to on the phone. My aunt rang her almost daily, and my other aunt, her brother's wife from Wembley too would call her at least once a week, and mum would have a conversation with them, clearly aware of who she was talking with.

My sister-in-law, Bina, would ring my mum every evening, before mum's bed time to make sure that she was okay. My mum would thank her for thinking of her and end the conversation by saying that she should ring her every night, in case she had died, and her body undiscovered for days. Then she would say that it wouldn't matter to her, as she would be dead, but people would talk about the daughters-in-laws for not caring. She repeated the same last words at the end of the conversation every time.

This had played in her mind from the day, when a few years back, just before Christmas, I had gone to see her and found that the old man who lived below her flat had not collected his mail for several days and it was piling up. She shared the main door with him, then upon entering the main door there were their individual doors to their flats.

We put it down to him being away to see family over Christmas. But the next visit to my mum, I found yet more mail, put though the main door.

I decided to press the emergency call button, in my mum's flat. When it was answered, I told them that my mum was fine, but that I was worried about the gentleman downstairs, as he had not collected his mail for two weeks.

They decided to ring his family, as they always had a couple of family member's numbers on their records.

Soon an ambulance and a police car arrived, and they had to break down the door. They were met by a decomposed dead body of the neighbour in his flat.

When the door was opened, there was a stench of the corpse coming out of his flat.

My mum was horrified and disturbed by the incident and was surprised that his family members had not got in touch with him, over the two weeks, or perhaps more. Surely, they would have rung him at some stage, and worried if he hadn't answered the phone.

This incident always played in my mum's head. This was the reason, for her asking my sisters-in-law to ring her daily.

She would always tell us to ring her often, to make sure she was alright.

There were times when there was no answer, when we rang her. We would try ringing a bit later, thinking that she might be asleep, or in the bathroom, but when she wouldn't answer her phone after numerous calls to her, we would panic that she might have fallen down, or the worst could have happened, so me being the nearest to her flat, would drive to her flat to check if she was alright.

Most of the times, she would not have answered the call because she had not placed the telephone receiver down properly.

So, the rushed journey would be a waste of time, though, she would be glad that she had an unplanned company.

On occasions, before her illness, if we couldn't get hold of her, we would ring our aunty Kamala, to see if my mum was with her. Most of the times, she was, but if she wasn't, we would panic and then our aunty would drive to her flat to check on her.

A new neighbour had moved into the flat below, which gave us a bit of reassurance.

He was a gentleman, and was always happy to help whenever he could. He would place our mum's post through her letterbox, and keep an eye on the people's movement, coming and going out of her flat. He had a perfect view point out of his front window of the front of the flat. In fact, he got familiar with everyone, and was always able to spot a stranger. Since my mum never answered her door, he would come out, see to the people at the main entrance door, and deal with them accordingly.

Our mum's health was going downhill. There were more and more hospital visits. She was often constipated and always in so much pain, so the carers would call an ambulance for her, and she would end up in A&E. The doctors had found her having kidney stones, but did not want to operate on her, due to her age, as she approached her 94th birthday. So, they would treat her by giving her laxatives and painkillers and put her on a drip in order to hydrate her.

It would be so sad to see her scream with pain.

After her treatment, we would take her back home. But the same would occur again and again, and she would be back in hospital.

Several times, I took my aunty to the hospital to visit my mum. She too complained that her health was not like it used to be. She always felt lethargic, and her legs were always in so much pain that she found walking difficult. The doctors were doing several tests on her, but had not worked out whatever was wrong with her.

Mum's visits became so regular, that we got to know the A&E staff well.

From the start of the year 2019, our mum started getting worse. All the family were taking turns to visit her. Even the grandchildren started visiting her, whenever they were in the area. Since she had had a fall from her bed, and had lain on the floor till the morning carer came in, she always complained of the pain in her arm. She could not raise it when being dressed.

Overall, she was in pain in almost all parts of her body.

On Friday 22nd on the March of 2019, I got a call from the morning carer to say that my mum was in a very bad condition and she had sent for an ambulance.

The ambulance staff did some tests on her and had to get in touch with her doctor to update them of her condition.

Her blood sugar had drastically gone down, so we were advised to take her to the hospital to be put on a drip.

She was once again taken to her regular hospital which was West Middlesex hospital.

Our mum hated the sight of hospitals, especially the West Middlesex, as this was where our dad had passed away.

Most of us siblings ended up at the hospital, to visit her since it was the weekend.

After various tests and scans, the doctors advised that she should be admitted to the ICU.

She was very scared and worried, when she ended up in ICU, as most of the patients, in the ward were very ill. She would watch them, and ask us if she was going to end up like them.

We reassured her that she was in the right place, and that the doctors were going to make her feel better.

She was taken good care of, but was always in so much pain, due to the kidney stones. She would scream in pain, when the nurses tried to give her a bed bath or change her. Sometimes she was abusive to the nurses, accusing them of hurting her.

Whenever I went to visit mum, she would plead with me to take her back home. She said that she did not want to stay in hospital. I was so helpless and saddened that I could not fulfil her wish.

Her health was getting worse by the day. She was being given morphine in order to ease her pain.

She would hardly eat her food, and was forever sleeping, with her hot water bottle by her side.

While she was in hospital, my brothers, Gulab and Ashok, were trying hard to find her a care home, for we realised that she needed 24 -hour care now.

They visited several care homes in the vicinity of her house, till they came across a suitable place not far from the West Middlesex Hospital. They went to see the owner of the place, and started making arrangements to move our mum in.

One afternoon, when I went to visit my mum in the ICU, my sisters-in-law, who had been visiting my mum with my brothers, told me that my aunty had been admitted in a ward, just a few yards away from our mum's.

I went to visit her, where she was surround by my cousins. They told me that our aunt had been admitted in order to have tests to investigate her condition.

Our aunt did not want us to tell our mum, that she was there, in the same ward, to avoid upsetting her, and making her health worse. So despite being so close to each other, they did not see each other.

It was only when our mum was ready to be moved to the care home that my aunt went to see her briefly, from the isolation room, feet away from mum's ward.

The Care Home

Just after twelve days in the ICU, our mum was able to move into the care home. It was a Hospice.

Before she was taken there in an Ambulance, my brothers and sisters-in-law had placed most of her clothes and toiletries in her room. They had brought along with them the pictures of all the family members, in their frames and hung them on the walls, in order to familiarise her to her surroundings.

They had also taken her quilt and covers, to make her feel at home.

Her baby accompanied her too.

As the family made her comfortable in her new bed, she asked them if this was to be her new home!

The family members would visit her day and night. Madhu and Bina's younger sister, and her husband would bring freshly cooked food over to the Hospice, for mum and for whoever had come to visit her. The staff were kind enough to let us use their canteen to warm up the food, have our meals and the facilities of making tea or coffee.

They were glad that the family were visiting mum, as that made their job easy, for looking after patients who had no one visiting them.

Mum was not able to eat a lot by now. Just a few spoonfuls, was all she could manage.

We had kept her on going diary in her room, so that whoever visited her could leave a note in it of her well-being.

Harmesh and Margaret had also come over to see her and tried feeding her.

According to the notes in the diary, she was not eating or drinking much, she was refusing to take her tablets, and when the carers tried to feed her or wash her, she was shouting and often hitting or slapping them.

Her behaviour forced them to keep her sedated.

On the tenth day of her being in the hospice, I went to visit her and found her sleeping most of the time. I sat next to her on the bed and massaged her legs.

When the carer came over to feed her, she was unable to swallow her food. She was just holding her water in her mouth, and not able to swallow that either.

This really worried me, so I went to speak to the head nurse.

He told me that my mum was at the end of her life, and there was not much they could do now, but keep her as comfortable as possible.

Hearing his words, I realised how ill our mum was, and that she would never be going home.

I rang the family to tell them the bad news, which I'm sure they were aware of already, but were in denial, just as I was.

The next day, despite her own ill health, our aunty came to see our mum, brought over by my cousin since she had been discharged from hospital by now.

She had left a note in the diary, saying that my mum was fast asleep and was not opening her eyes. She was very sad to see her sister in this condition and not being able to have a conversation with her.

She wrote that she will pray for her and misses her, and that God bless her.

That evening Ashok and Bina came over, and found that our mum was nor responding at all. All she was doing was sleeping.

Bina decided to stay by our mum's bed side, and I too stayed overnight with her, making makeshift beds, next to our mum, with the pillows and blankets the carers had provided us with.

One of the carers was kind enough to lend us a CD player, on which Bina would continually play some religious hymns. In case my mum could hear them. They were very soothing for us as well, playing softly in the background.

All the family were around mum's bed, talking to her all the time, hoping that she would open her eyes and respond to us. All she was doing was breathing so heavily that we could see her chest move up and down rapidly.

She was surrounded by all the family, along with the grandchildren, each one of us holding her hand and talking to her, her eyes would flicker under her eyelids a bit, but she would not open them.

Bina would stay with her every night, fulfilling our mum's wishes that she did not want to leave this world, with no one by her side.

I visited mum on the Good Friday Bank holiday, and Sirita visited her too. Bina's younder sister had once again brought some food for everyone, and we all went to the canteen and helped ourselves.

My brothers would stay at our mum's flat, so that they could easily travel daily to the Hospice.

Poly suggested that she wanted to stay the night by my mum's side with Bina, so on Saturday, I decided to have a break from visiting mum.

I got a call from family that evening, with sad news that our mum had passed away.

She died on Easter Saturday at 21.50 pm.

I rushed to the hospital in my car, hoping to have a last glimpse of mum, but she had already been taken away.

All my siblings and my dear sisters-in-law were there, in the family room. We all gave each other comfort.

Poly had jotted in my mum's Visitors' Diary, that night.

She was lying facing away from us.

She took two gargling breaths, and then passed away.

This was at 21.50

She looked very peaceful

Just when she passed away, there was sounds of fireworks (may be at the nearby Syon Park)

We all sat with her.

May she rest in peace!

When we think back, both Didi and our dad died during Easter time, and now our mum too.

The pillar holding the family together was no more!

We all went back to my mum's flat, exhausted from the day. We made make shift beds on the sofas, on the hospital bed, and on the living room floor, using quilts and beddings, that mum had stored away in her cupboards, in case we ever came to stay the night, and we all fell sleep.

Never had we been all together, sleeping in our mum's flat before.

It had always been her wish to have us all together in her flat, with her, for one night at least, but we always said to her that it was not practical and left her, making our way to our own homes.

And, now, we were all there fulfilling her wish, but she was not there!

The last entry in the Visitors' diary was made by Gulab on Easter Monday 22nd April 2019 -

No more pain

No more worries

Rest in peace with us and the world.

In the other world, have all your wishes fulfilled.

Hope we did right by you.

My brothers and sisters-in-law went back to the Hospice the next couple of days to sort out mum's belongings in her room. All her pyjama sets were left with the Hospice, to be used on patients, who had no family.

Most evenings, we would all gather at our mum's flat, as my brothers made arrangements for the funeral.

The rest of the family members and friends were also visiting us there, paying their respects.

Harmesh and Margaret came over from up North.

All my mum's grand children came too, and the flat was always full of people.

Sonal, Sirita, Richard, Amie and Holly too joined us a few evenings, and we would all share stories about our mum.

This made me realise how much she was respected by all the family members.

On the day of mum's funeral, held on 3rd May 2019, We all went to the Resting Chapel and had a traditional funerary ceremony, conducted by a Hindu Pandit.

Then the funeral was carried out in the afternoon, followed by her wake.

It was very dignified and smooth running.

All the uncles, aunts, cousins and family members were present, along with our cousin, Daisy, who had travelled all the way from Canada, and Madhu and Bina's brothers, one of whose wives, travelled all the way from Canada.

Our mum's flat became the hub of all the family, where we would gather and discuss the future of the flat, and all our mum's belongings.

Most of her belongings were distributed amongst the family members, but the rest was taken to the charity shops.

We also discussed about the journey to India, where my mum's ashes would have to be taken to Hardwar, on the Holy River Ganges, for that was her wish. That is where our dad's ashes were taken too. In fact, all the members of our family, who had departed previously had their ashes scattered in the Ganges, as per Hindu tradition. Their names added on the records of our forefathers, by the Pandits, on their death records.

Our dear mother had left all of us siblings a sufficient amount of money in her will. When I was given my share of the inheritance, I used part of it to purchase a new car.

Losing our beloved aunt

Not long after our mum's funeral, we had yet another sad news that our aunty had passed away too. She was the last of my mum's siblings. Aunty died of blood cancer, after a short term of suffering.

Our uncle had passed, many years before, so her six daughters arranged her funeral. It was all done in a very dignified manner. My cousins had to be very strong, losing their dear mum, and support each other, which they did.

We would always remember our aunty for she was there for us, during our childhood.

She was there for our mum too, when she was going through her illness.

She will be remembered for her strong and caring nature, for she was always coming to people's aid, when they needed her.

It was sad to know that the whole of our parents' generation was wiped out.

Our Trip to India

We were making plans for all of the siblings to make the journey to Haridwar, along with Bina and Madhu, which would give us all a chance to give our mum a dignified send-off, just as she had wished.

Sadly, our brother Harmesh, and sister-in-law, Margaret, were unable to accompany us.

A couple of months before we were to fly to India, there was news of a virus going on, believed to have started in Wuhan, in China, in December 2019.

The Covid-19 Pandemic, known as the Corona Virus, was caused by Severe Acute Respiratory Syndrome.

The media and the news casters were on the news every hour giving accounts of the Covid -19 spreading to other countries.

Some of the cruise ships were stranded at ports not allowing passengers to disembark, fearing that they may be carrying the Virus, brought from countries they had visited, as some cases were reported of people being sick on board the boats.

Panic was setting in and the public were asked to wash their hands as often as possible.

Soon sanitising gels were recommended, and that soon became very hard to get hold of, due to the demand.

We were pleased that our flight to India had not been cancelled, and we would be able to travel still. I was worried about my chronic cough, in case people mistook it for Corona Virus, as that was one of the symptoms of the deadly virus.

After all our travelling planes were finalised, and the tickets booked, we all set off for India on Friday 21st February 2020.

Poly and I had travelled to Heathrow Airport, and were waiting for my brothers and sisters-in-law to get there, when I saw them all walking towards us. Ashok had a bag in his hand, and he said that our mum was travelling with us. The bag had my mum's ashes in an urn.

That brought a lump to my throat. Thinking how elated she would have been, if all of us were travelling to India with her, when she was alive.

My last time in India was in the year 1981, so I was excited to be travelling there with my siblings.

We reached Delhi Airport on February 22nd, and then boarded a train to take us to Haridwar, where we were met by our guide who had made all the transport arrangements and had also arranged the Pandits who were to perform the ceremony.

The whole of the funerary ceremony was a very sad occasion, we comforted each other and the ceremony went very smoothly.

We had given our mum a send-off that she deserved.

That afternoon we took a train to Jalandhar, the city where I had come to my in-laws with Arun, Sonal and Sirita.

It looked very modern and different to what I had seen almost 39 years ago.

The next day, we took a taxi to Dasia, to our mum's village, where she had been brought up. Gulab had childhood memories of the place, when he was a young boy, and his wish was to have a last look of the village my mum grew up in.

We were driven through muddy roads, with farms on both sides of the road, with their lush crops of ripe yellow mustard, sugarcane and various other crops, as far as the eye could see.

We asked the locals around, as to where our mum's relatives lived, and they were able to point out to us the street where they lived.

They were not expecting us, but welcomed us with open arms, when we told them of our family connection. They happened to be the third generation of our mum's family, so had heard about my mum and uncle, but we were strangers to them.

They showed us around the house. Unfortunately it was not the original house where our mum would have lived, even though the original house was still there, right next to theirs, with just a couple of walls still standing, and was in ruins, with rubble and old bricks surrounding it.

I am not sure of the rest of the family, but I somehow got comfort being in the place where my mum had been brought up.

I could just visualize her helping her mum with the chores, and sitting there with her mum's spinning wheel, weaving, knitting and making dolls out of clay. And tending to her young siblings. All the things she would tell me stories about, of her childhood.

My brothers and sisters-in-law's wish was to donate some money to the local school in Dasia.

Our relatives rushed us to the school, which happened to be about a fifteen- minute walk away from their house, as we only had limited time, before the school would close.

Once again, we were welcome by the head of the school and all the young students, who took pleasure in sharing my sunglasses with me, and posing for the pictures we took of them. Bina spoiled them by handing out some sweets. She had also donated some pencils, pens and books.

It was a basic village school with a handful of classes with a blackboard, and all the students sat on mats on the floor.

The school time was almost over, so we headed back to our relatives' house. On the way there, I noticed how the little shops, the houses and the streets were still very traditional. They had water pumps in the streets, and we all took pleasure in pumping them, and having pictures taken. Some of the local old men were sat outside their doorways, and looked at us messing around, I guess wondering what the fascination was.

As we returned to the house, the ladies of the house had prepared a meal for us of saag and Makkai Roti. Which was a traditional corn bread to be had with spinach, and with a drink of yogurt (lassi).

We all sat on their patio to have the delicious meal, only yards away from where my mum had lived her childhood. It all seemed so surreal.

Gulab had vivid memories of the village during his childhood. He asked our relatives to take him to the man-made lake, where he had played with his friends, in his youth. He got a ride on the back of a motorbike to the lake. Upon seeing the lake, Gulab thought that it looked smaller than how he remembered it. He was pleased that we had visited Dasia, and was overwhelmed and emotional talking about it.

After our goodbyes and farewells, and all the formalities of thanking our kind relatives for their hospitality, we took a taxi to Amritsar, where we were to stay in a hotel for three nights.

We had a great time eating in traditional Dhaba's and shopping in shops selling vibrant coloured clothes and wares.

We also visited the Golden Temple, the gurudwara, which is a spiritual site of Sikhism. The temple's amazing architecture, the pure 24 carat gold decoration and the man-made pool, all added to its glory. The history of the Golden Temple fascinated me.

We walked around the temple, and found peace of mind, hearing the chants of the worshippers in the background.

The family made a donation on behalf of our late mum, and ended our stay at the gurudwara after a Langar.

We also got a chance to visit Beating the Retreat Ceremony, held at the Wagah Border of Amritsar and Lahore, held every evening, where both the Indian and Pakistani military displayed their showmanship.

It was very colourful, at times an amusing ceremony, the way both parties tried to compete, displaying their best moves. This ceremony normally ended with the closing of the border gates and lowering of the flags.

That evening we decided to go for a walk and check out how far the Amritsar train station was from our hotel, so we could plan our times for the next morning for our train that would take us to Mumbai.

Luckily, it wasn't far at all. We decided to walk into the station, to check out the trains.

As we stood at the platform, the announcement on the Tannoy was of the approaching train. I got my phone out, ready to record the arrival of the train. I was amazed at the majestic size of the engine as it approached the platform, followed by a trail of carriages. It took two minutes before the train came to a standstill, and yet there were more carriages beyond, where I stood to do the recording. It was a very long train, and I was excited to know that we would be travelling on one such train the next morning to Mumbai.

After three amazing days in Amritsar, we took an overnight train to Mumbai which was to be the last stop of our trip.

It was a fascinating sight, when passing through villages, the rivers and beautiful sceneries of India, as well as the shanty towns and farms and the way of life of the poor families living at the edge of the railway lines. Young children giving us a wave, as if they knew us, the sound of the majestic train's wheels against the rails, the sound of the engine, and the occasional whistle brought back memories of the journeys we used to make with our parents years ago. It was like a deja-vu.

We would purchase some local food and tea from the vendors, when the train would stop at the stations.

We had two compartments to share amongst ourselves, so we would gather in one of them and talk for hours of our experiences of the journey.

We would talk about the places we had either stopped at or passed on our journey, about the stories of the places we had heard of from our parents.

When the night fell, we all settled on to our pull-out bunk beds, settling into our sleep with the judder of the train. In the morning my brother, Ashok, announced that I had missed the stop of my birth place "Karnal" as we had passed it in the middle of the night. I would have loved to have had a glimpse of the station, at least.

MUMBAI

Our train stopped at the Mumbai Station. Once again this was an enormous station, lined up with long trains on the platforms. People hurrying up to-and-fro, either boarding them or arriving. We hired some Rickshaws to take us along with our luggage to our hotel, which was not far from the station.

We stayed at yet another luxurious hotel, which Ashok was familiar with, as he had stayed at it, on one of his previous trips to India.

We settled down, and then ventured out to see the sights of Mumbai.

We went for a walk on the famous Juhu beach, after having had our lunch. Ashok had a massage done on the beach while we watched him being kneaded and cupped, with a special massage oil. He also had his head massaged, and seemed to be in heaven, from the look on his face.

We returned to the beach, in the evening too, where there were hundreds of people eating, drinking and having fun. There were youngsters playing cricket on the beach, one of the most common pastimes of Indians.

We only had two days left, for our trip to come to an end.

The next morning, we ventured out to Santa Cruz, to an area, where most of the Bollywood stars resided.

We walked on the street, where a famous Bollywood star Amitabh Bachchan lived. We were hoping to have a glimpse of him, as it was known that at certain times of the day, he would step out of his mansion to greet people. The security guards at the gate told us that we were too early for that. We were not prepared to hang around, so didn't get to see him.

During our walk in the crowded streets, we sampled the coconut water out of fresh coconuts. And also sugarcane juice, which was prepared by the vendors, using an iron mangle to press out the delicious juices.

Ashok announced that evening that we were to leave the hotel the next morning, and make arrangements for another hotel, for our last night, so that we would be nearer to the airport. The next morning, we checked out of our hotel.

We were picked up by a couple of taxis to take us to the new hotel.

Ashok, Bina, Poly and I took one taxi and Gulab and Madhu were in the second one.

It was a journey that took us along the Mumbai Trans Harbour link.

As we approached the hotel, a hotel attendant came and opened our car doors and welcomed us. I looked up at the vast hotel, and to my surprise it was the famous 'TAJ'.

Yes! We were at the Taj hotel. I couldn't contain my excitement as we walked into the hotel.

As we entered the foyer, we were greeted by smartly dressed Indian ladies in their silk saris. They placed a garland around our necks and put a tikka on our forehead, as a welcome gesture.

I was so excited and overwhelmed to be staying in such a posh hotel.

I had watched documentaries and some programmes about the famous Taj hotel, and was fascinated about it.

Ashok told us that this was to be a treat for us all from Gulab, as he and Madhu had stayed here before on one of their holidays, and wanted the rest of us to experience the stay at this famous hotel.

Minutes later, Gulab, with Madhu, arrived at the foyer, a big smile on his face, when he saw how excited and grateful we were to him, but all he said to us was that the pleasure was all his.

We were shown to our rooms. I was to share a room with Poly. As we entered the room, there were various colours of balloons neatly scattered all over the floor and the bed, and a welcoming bowl of exotic fruit waiting for us.

There were petals neatly placed on the bath tub ledge and some outside of the marble bathroom.

The view from our window was of the back of the hotel, where there was the swimming pool.

Gulab had arranged birthday treats for Bina and me, so we were presented with delicious cakes in our rooms, which we all got together to share and enjoy.

We all decided to get changed and have a dip in the swimming pool. There was an area by the pool, where there were easels and paper laid out for people who would want to have a go at some drawing and art.

Ashok and I did a picture each. His was much better than my attempt.

We were shown around the hotel by a guide, and it was fascinating to learn about the history of the hotel. We were also told about the 2008 Mumbai attacks that took place at the Taj, by Islamist terrorists where 21 people were killed and 28 injured.

There was a shrine created in one part of the hotel to remember the deceased.

They showed us how the parts of the hotel that had been destroyed, had been restored to perfection.

We were invited to a high tea, followed by a magnificent dinner in the evening.

Unfortunately the stay at the Taj had come to an end and the next morning we left for the airport after an amazing experience.

There were two posh cars, with smartly dressed chauffeurs that picked us up from the front of the hotel and drove us to the airport.

Our amazing journey to India was almost at its end.

This amazing experience brought all of us siblings, and our sisters-in-law very close.

Over the duration of our trip, there were no disagreements or arguments, amongst the siblings.

Just laughter, enjoyment, eating, having fun, sharing and most of all respect for each other.

We were all overwhelmed by Gulab's generosity, and couldn't thank him enough for an amazing treat.

The Pandemic

There was a lot of talk of Covid-19 on the plane, and we were worried, that we might be stopped by the airport authorities and quarantined, due to our travel to India.

Luckily, we just sailed through the airport without any complication.

Upon our arrival, I returned to work and business was as usual.

There was a lot on the news about people dying of Covid-19, in hospitals and care homes.

Most of the hospitals were overwhelmed with patients, and the non-urgent cases were being cancelled.

Soon there was talk of introduction of urgent PPI, for hospitals and care homes, and the demand could not be met.

Then on March 23rd 2020, the Prime Minister, Boris Johnson, announced that there was to be a lockdown.

No one was allowed to return to work, and wherever possible, people were encouraged to work from home. People were only allowed out for a short walk. Most of the restaurants, pubs, dentists, hairdressers, and more or less all the non-essential shops had to close down in order to avoid the virus spreading.

All the schools closed down, and the students were given lessons, online, by their teachers or by parents wherever possible. Some families, that could not afford computers or laptops, were donated with new or second-hand ones by public, or authorities.

This also meant that I could no longer work.

The airports were shut down, the buses as well as the railways, stopped from operating.

Wearing masks became compulsory in the shops, hospitals and public places.

We considered ourselves lucky, to have been able to return to UK from India in good time, as some people were stranded all over the world, not being able to get flights back.

The supermarkets had marked distances of three meters, on their entrance floors and the aisles in order for people to keep their distance from each other. There would be long queues at the supermarkets, and people were rationed to fewer items of essentials, like toilet rolls, pasta and flour.

There were sanitising machines installed everywhere for people to use.

The supermarket trolleys were sanitised after every use, by the supermarket staff, to avoid the virus spreading.

The tourism and hospitality sector suffered, as all the hotels and the holiday resorts were shut down.

Weddings, or any kind of celebration couldn't take place, and people were cancelling their forthcoming weddings.

People just stayed indoors, unless they needed to get their shopping.

Some volunteers were kind enough to deliver food to the elderly and vulnerable, to their door step. Most of the supermarkets introduced a home delivery system that had to be booked, days in advance.

There was nothing to do, and nowhere to go, for every amenity had been shut down.

Alan and I would go for walks to Windsor town and back in order to stretch our legs. The roads were empty with hardly any cars on the roads. The streets were like a ghost town.

The sad sights we witnessed on our walks was the disposal of used masks and rubber gloves in the streets, by some careless and thoughtless people.

On our walks, we would witness ambulances whizzing past us, as we walked, with most probably Covid patients on their way to already overflown Covid wards.

People spent their days, watching the daily bulletins on the television, run by the Prime Minister, Boris Johnson, and medical professionals, updating the public of the latest news of the Covid-19.

The hospitals were overflowing with Covid patients, and the doctors and nurses were working day and night trying to keep the patients as comfortable as possible, with supplies often running low. They had a tough job at their hand.

The NHS was bursting at its seams, and care homes were struggling too.

Families could not visit their loved ones in the care homes, and unfortunately, some patients died, without seeing their loved ones.

Funerals were also limited to just the immediate family.

The funeral parlours and the morgues were overloaded with dead bodies, so the corpses were kept in refrigerated lorry containers.

It was not just in England, the virus was spreading fast all over the world, and the entire world was going through the pandemic.

We were unable to see family members, so we would have Zoom meetings, regularly, amongst all the siblings, and update each other on our lives in a lockdown.

We started spending a lot of time in our gardens, and we would send pictures of our creations to each other on WhatsApp.

Medical scientists all over the globe were trying to develop a vaccine to combat the fast spreading virus.

Then on 2nd December 2020, the Pfizer-BioNTech Covid-19 vaccine was approved in UK, becoming the first to be authorised to be used anywhere in the world.

The very first vaccine was administered to a patient in UK on the 8th Dec 2020, at Guys Hospital.

Soon every person was given the jab. In fact they were to get a booster jab.

There were centres set up all over the country for the public to have their vaccine-jabs.

The vaccine was proving to be working, so the lockdown was eased on 1ST June 2020.

Some of the people returned to work, some of the shops opened. The garden centres were getting busy again, and thus, there was a bit of normality returning, all around. The schools were open, and students were returning back to their schools and universities.

I could have returned to work, but most of my clients were happy for me not to return, as there were still cases of Covid-19 present.

I had two families that were happy to have me return to work, provided I was kitted with PPI.

As the month of September approached, at the age of 66, I took my retirement, on 20th September 2020. I no longer returned to work. I was very excited, when I received my bus pass. Though I was not able to use it, due to the lockdown, I was looking forward to using it when things returned to normal.

Then the second lockdown was announced on 31st October 2020. But this time some manufacturing companies, and building sites were allowed to carry on working.

People were to stay in a bubble, and not mix, outside of their bubble, small wedding ceremonies, and funerals could take place. Pubs and restaurants were allowed to run a takeaway service only. All these precautions were taken to slow down the spread of the deadly virus.

In March 2020, the Chancellor, Rishi Sunak launched a furlough scheme, that would help businesses and the employers pay their workers majority of their wages, due to having to shut their business down. The self- employed were also given a grant to subsidise their loss of earnings.

I was lucky enough to receive this grant.

Our Egyptian Experience Apartment

We had many numerous holidays to our apartment in Egypt, and many happy times. But we soon stopped going there after the flights to Sharm-el-Sheikh were halted in November 2015, for at least four years, after the bombing of a Russian plane, by the militant group ISIS, which killed all the 224 people on board.

The apartment was not being used, and we were not sure when we would be able to go there again.

Then in 2020, we went through the lockdown.

This is when Alan decided that we sell the apartment.

One of the staff members at the Egyptian Experience Complex helped us towards the sale of the apartment.

We heard that most of the owners at this complex had sold or rented out their apartments.

The Death of Prince Philip the Duke of Edinburgh

The Queen of United Kingdom, Elizabeth II, resided at the Windsor Castle, during the duration of Covid-19 lockdown. All her duties were to be carried out from the castle.

In February 2021, it was announced that the Duke of Edinburgh, Prince Philip, had been hospitalised, after feeling unwell. He was released from hospital after 23 days, after receiving treatment.

Unfortunately, the news of Prince Philip's death was announced on 9th of April 2021. He died at the age of 99.

His funeral took place on 17th April 2021 at Windsor Castle. It was televised for the public to see.

It was so sad to see the Queen, sat by herself with a mask on, as the funeral service took place, adhering to the Covid-19 rules.

The funeral service was held at St George's Chapel, by the Dean of Windsor.

His coffin was laid at the Royal Vault in Windsor.

Living with Covid-19

With most of the country, having being vaccinated against Covid-19, and having received at least three doses, the death rates were tremendously falling down, and people were recovering well, by just isolating at home, rather than having to end up in hospitals.

Covid-19, slowly but surely was at last under control.

In February 2022 the Prime Minister, Boris Johnson set out plans for Living with Covid.

All the restrictions were lifted. The Booster Vaccines were to be introduced in order to manage the virus.

All the businesses started up as normal, weddings and funerals could be held, as in pre-Covid times.

People started going on holidays, as the planes started flying.

It was all back to normal though there were still cases of Covid around.

Boris Johnson

There had been a lot of controversy going on about the state of the country under Boris Johnson's leadership. Some of his own members were complaining about him, for breaking Covid and lockdown rules, and misleading the Parliament.

He had been having drinking parties, and had been breaking rules about social distancing, that he had set himself.

Over the months, when Russia and Ukraine went into war, the cost of living went up. Petrol, gas and electricity prices shot up.

It was time for a change in the government and Liz Truss, the previous Secretary of state for Foreign, Commonwealth and Development Affairs, and Rishi Sunak, the Chancellor of Exchequer were the candidates chosen to be elected.

Prime Minister, Boris Johnson, resigned on 5th September 2022.

On 6th September 2022, Liz Truss was elected as the new Prime Minister of the United Kingdom. She visited the Queen at Balmoral, where she was asked to form a new government.

She moved into 10 Downing Street on 8th September.

The Queen Elizabeth II

Since the death of Prince Philips, the Duke of Edinburgh, the Queen was attending fewer and fewer appointments and occasions, as her health was deteriorating. Prince Charles would attend to the appointments she was unable to keep.

She moved to her Scottish Balmoral Castle, where she often spent part of her summer break.

The Queen had served the nation and the Commonwealth for 75 years. She was the first ever monarch to celebrate her Platinum Jubilee.

She became the Queen after the death of her father King George VI and came to the throne in 1952 at the age of 25.

On September 8th 2022 the news hit the nation that the Queen had died peacefully at her Balmoral Castle.

The whole nation was in mourning. Thousands of people travelled to Buckingham palace, the Windsor castle and other Royal residences to place flowers, and paid their respects.

When her coffin was laid at Westminster Abbey, thousands of people lined up the streets to pay their last respects.

Wherever the coffin was taken, thousands of mourners queued for hours to have a glimpse of her coffin and pay their respects.

All the funerary services and the funeral was done in a very dignified manner.

After the death of the beloved Queen, Prince Charles became the future King, and was given the title of King Charles III, and the Duchess was to become the Queen Consort.

The Queen had always given a speech to the public at Christmas, every year.

In 1992 in her speech she had said that the year 1992 was "annus horribilis" for her.

There had been the fire at Windsor Castle that destroyed part of the castle, Princess Diana's and Prince Charles' relationship, and the divorce of three of her sons had contributed to her bad year.

The year 2022 turned out be "annus horribilis" for the nation, and the Royal family.

EPILOGUE

I was inspired by my friends and family to write my memoirs. As I spoke to them of my life experiences, they would encourage me to put my stories on paper. I would jot notes on my phone and in a note book, of the things I wanted to write in my book, for years, but did not start writing till I retired.

It has been a very slow process, as I am not a touch typist or tech-savvy.

I give thanks to my daughter Sirita for all advice and shortcuts she has taught me, to write my book.

I also thank my husband, Alan, for being patient with me, when I would isolate myself in order to have peace whilst writing.

My book is full of humour, heartbreak, and adventure, and I would not want to change anything I have gone through, as all my experiences have made me the person that I am today.

I am content with my life. I am happily married. My daughters are doing well in work and life.

After years of living in a rental property, Sirita bought her first duplex flat in Bracknell.

I am very proud of her, for working hard to achieve her dream.

My granddaughter, Holly, is doing well in her studies, and Amie is in a great job, and also on the verge of going on the property ladder, and has put a deposit on a property with her partner, James.

There is nothing more I would ask for.

Milton Keynes UK
Ingram Content Group UK Ltd.
UKHW020208230823
427286UK00018B/854